FOR VALOUR

West Country VCs

EV Thompson

Published by Truran 2004

Truran is an imprint of Truran Books Ltd
Croft Prince, Mount Hawke, Truro, Cornwall TR4 8EE
www.truranbooks.co.uk

© EV Thompson 2004
ISBN 1 85022 185 5

Printed and bound in Cornwall by R. Booth Ltd
Antron Hill, Mabe, Penryn, Cornwall TR10 9HH

Acknowledgments

The author would like to thank David Raw for permission to quote from his book, *It's Only Me*, the very moving story of Reverend Theodore Bayley Hardy, VC, DSO, MC and for the photograph of Hardy. The staff of the DCLI Museum, Bodmin, Cornwall for their unstinting help with photographs and material from their archives, with particular thanks to Roy Prince for his help and enthusiasm; the Devonshire and Dorset Regiment Charitable Trust for permission to use material held at the Keep Military Museum, Dorchester and the photograph of a portrait of Corporal TWH Veale, VC; soldiers of Gloucestershire Museum, Gloucester, for details and photograph of Colonel JP Carne, VC, DSO; the Victoria Cross Society who provided a great many photographs from their extensive collection; the East Lancs Museum for photographs and material in respect of Lieutenant Colonel Ervine-Andrews, VC; Brian Coode, for allowing me to view family photographs and personal papers in respect of Lieutenant T Melvill, VC; Mrs Frances Stephens, churchwarden of St Winnow; the Royal Navy Museum, Portsmouth; the Museum of Lincolnshire Life; the Cornwall Centre, Redruth; the Cornwall Family History Society and the curators and staff of many other museums, together with individuals in Devon and Cornwall whose help and enthusiasm has been invaluable in obtaining material for this book of West Country heroes.

The cover picture is taken from a painting of Ervine-Andrews, winning the only VC at Dunkirk, by Frank Wootton commissioned by the East Lancashire Regiment and now displayed in the officers' mess of the Queen's Lancashire Regiment. Back cover photograph of William Dowling's VC medal by Barry Yelland.

Contents

The Victoria Cross

The Victoria Cross is unquestionably the most exclusive and prestigious decoration for valour in the whole of the world and recognised as such by those who collect medals awarded for outstanding acts of bravery.

The award was founded by Queen Victoria, on 29th January, 1856, as a reward to serving members of the Royal Navy and the British Army who had performed an outstanding act of valour in the presence of the enemy.

The Victoria Cross – the 'VC' –is not an order, such as that of the Garter, but is intended as a decoration, superior to all other awards, bestowed upon either officers or men, whose actions put them above all distinctions of rank.

In the early years, a number of recipients were stripped of the award when later found guilty of disreputable conduct but King George V, grandson of the decoration's founder, declared that, 'No matter the crime committed by anyone on whom the VC has been conferred, the decoration should not be forfeited. Even were a VC to be sentenced to be hanged for murder, he should be allowed to wear his VC upon the scaffold.'

In 1902, King Edward VII approved the principle of awarding the VC posthumously. This was confirmed in 1907 and made retrospective to 1856. However, many very brave acts went unrecognised because the men who performed them had died as a result of their bravery and, aware the VC could not then be awarded posthumously, no recommendation had been made.

Nevertheless, this most prestigious award has been given to 1,354 recipients in the century-and-a-half that the award has been in existence. Of this number many had strong associations with the counties of Cornwall and Devon. Few would deny that the awards were justly earned and, in many cases, the recipients gave their lives in winning this token of Great Britain's recognition of their supreme bravery.

This small book details the deeds of a cross section of these very brave men who had strong West Country connections and whose actions earned them this decoration, awarded 'For Valour'. It does not claim to be a comprehensive register, but I hope it helps to demonstrate that any man entitled to wear the blue or crimson ribbon (before 1918 the ribbons of VCs awarded to naval personnel were blue) on the left breast of his uniform possessed a courage that has placed him among the greatest heroes of all time.

Joseph Trewavas 1835–1905

Trewavas was born on 14th December, 1835 in the small Cornish fishing village of Mousehole and seemed destined to follow his contemporaries into life as a fisherman. However, unlike many of the Mousehole boys of his day, Joseph received an education at the school in the nearby parish of Paul.

Perhaps it was here that his imagination was fired by history lessons telling of the British navy's pursuit of the Spaniards who landed in this small corner of the British Isles in 1595, setting fire to the church and many nearby properties and terrorising the Cornish inhabitants.

Whatever it was that caused him to change his destiny, Trewavas left his small and insular village when he was seventeen years of age and joined the Royal Navy.

In October 1853, he was posted to HMS *Agamemnon*, a revolutionary 91-gun ship of the line, described as a 'steam powered sailing ship' and sailed with the vessel to the Crimea in 1854. In October of that year Trewavas joined the Naval Brigade, landing with them to fight alongside the army in the atrocious conditions facing the British forces who with their French allies, were investing the Russian seaport city of Sebastopol.

He was there when British cavalrymen took part in a magnificent yet unnecessary and disastrous action that would be glorified in military history as 'The Charge of the Light Brigade'.

Less than a fortnight after this action Trewavas and the Naval Brigade took part in the battle of Inkerman, in which French and British forces fought off an attack by the Russian army, inflicting some 15,000 casualties upon them.

Surviving a disastrous winter which caused the deaths of thousands of British soldiers due to disease and exposure, Trewavas was sent on loan to HMS *Beagle* (commanded by a Lieutenant Hewett, who had himself performed an act of great bravery for which he would later receive a Victoria Cross). On this ship Trewavas would earn himself an honoured place amongst the bravest of the brave.

Beagle was sent to the Straits of Genitchi in the Sea of Azov where the Russian forces in the area were being supplied by a heavily defended pontoon bridge across the Straits which saved them an overland journey of more than 150 kilometres.

The captain of the *Beagle* received orders that the bridge was to be

*Joseph
Trewavas*

destroyed 'at all costs'. In view of this, three determined attempts were made on the bridge – the first led by the *Beagle's* commanding officer himself, but all the attempts failed, due to the extremely strong and determined enemy defences.

However, the captain of *Beagle* had his orders and a further attempt was made by Trewavas and four companions.

They set out for the pontoon bridge from *Beagle* in a small gig on 3rd July, 1855, watched in increasing disbelief by the hundreds of Russian troops who manned both shores. They could not believe that such a tiny force was making a serious attempt to destroy the bridge.

Nevertheless, when Joseph Trewavas leaped from the boat to the pontoon bridge and began hacking with an axe at the hawsers which held the pontoons together, the Russians were forced to take the attempt seriously and they opened a furious fire upon the young Cornishman.

Despite the murderous fire from both banks, Trewavas succeeded in cutting the hawsers holding the pontoons together and, as they drifted apart, he leaped back into the boat.

It was here that Trewavas's luck temporarily deserted him. A musket ball struck him in the shoulder and as the desperate oarsmen pulled towards the waiting Beagle the gig was so riddled with bullets that by the time it bumped against the side of the mother ship it was settling low in the water and ready to sink.

The wounded Trewavas was helped on board the ship and for this fearless feat would be awarded one of the very early VCs. He was also awarded the Conspicuous Gallantry Medal (CGM) and an admiring French nation awarded him their prestigious Legion of Honour.

By November 1855, Trewavas was well enough to return to HMS *Agamemnon* and in 1857, was presented with the Victoria Cross by the Queen herself, at an investiture in Hyde Park.

In the ensuing years Trewavas saw more action with the Royal Navy, serving in the East Indies and also in New Zealand during the Maori wars, but in 1862 this unassuming hero left the navy and returned to his native Mousehole.

Here he married Margaret Harry and together they raised a family of a boy, Joseph, and two daughters, Margaret and Elizabeth.

Trewavas never became a rich man, although he was able to purchase his own fishing boat – which he named *Agamemnon* – and also became a respected member of the community, serving on the Cornwall County Council in various committees. He was given an entry in *Who's Who* but, when asked to list his hobbies, replied that he was too busy earning a living to have any!

Sadly, late in life Trewavas was stricken with a paralysis which so depressed him that on 19th July, 1905, he attempted to cut his throat with a cheese knife and died the following day. A coroner recorded a verdict that he committed suicide while of unsound mind.

Joseph Trewavas was sixty-nine years of age when he died and although it is said that 2000 people attended his funeral at Paul church, no headstone was raised to mark his grave. The last resting place of this Cornish hero became lost until, in 1998, the detective work of dogged Cornish historian, Peter Waverly discovered its whereabouts only a short distance from the school attended by Joseph Trewavas, VC, CGM, when he was a young boy.

Harold Marcus Ervine-Andrews 1911–1995

Harold Marcus Ervine-Andrews was not a Cornishman by birth. He was, in fact, an Irishman, born in Cavan. However, after retiring from the army and spending a while in Devon, he moved to a quiet valley home in Cornwall. Here he lived out the last years of his life in an environment far removed from the action in which he won his Victoria Cross.

It is the lot of few men, or women, to look back on their life and say, 'By my actions I possibly changed the course of history' – and Lieutenant Colonel Ervine-Andrews, VC was a modest man who would certainly not have made such a claim …. but let the facts speak for themselves.

In May, 1940, the seemingly invincible German army was overrunning Europe and the retreating British army in France was in dire straits. Holland and Belgium had capitulated and a quarter-of-a-million British soldiers were trapped inside a shrinking perimeter centred upon the small French port of Dunkirk.

Resistance of any real substance had crumbled and the victorious German army was advancing, confident of taking prisoner the remnants of the British Expeditionary Force.

Lieutenant – acting Captain – Ervine-Andrews was commanding B Company of the 1st Battalion, East Lancashire Regiment, which been fighting a rearguard action against the advancing German army for ten days. His men were close to exhaustion and had suffered substantial casualties, but their war was far from over.

When B Company arrived at Dunkirk, the Commanding Officer of the 1st Battalion sent for Ervine-Andrews and wasted few words in explanation. 'There's a gap forming at the front and we've got to plug it. How many of your men can you get together?'

Despite his weariness, Ervine-Andrews replied, 'I suppose I've got sixty or seventy left of the company – but we're desperately short of ammunition.'

'We'll find what ammo we can for you. You're going back to the Canal de Bergues – tonight,' the Commanding Officer said tersely.

Returning to his Company, Ervine-Andrews had no illusions about what he and his men would be facing.

That night, leading his depleted Company back to the line of the canal, Ervine-Andrews reached his destination at about midnight. After putting the men into the best possible defensive position, he tried to snatch a couple of hours sleep, knowing full well there would be a very serious German attack in the morning.

Sure enough, the Germans attacked at dawn, in the words of Ervine-Andrews, 'throwing everything at us.'

The men of B Company doggedly held on to their position, but during the chaotic retreat through France their ammunition had either been dumped, lost, or gone astray and soon they were down to 50 or 60 rounds per man. It was an amount that automatic weapons would run away with in a few minutes.

Ervine-Andrews sent a desperate plea to his commanding officer for more ammunition with the result that every possible source was tried, even the bodies of dead soldiers being searched. Eventually, three Bren gun carriers were despatched to B Company with all the ammunition that could be mustered.

With the ammunition came an order from the Commanding Officer. Every minute gained was absolutely vital for the planned evacuation of the British army. B Company was to hang on for as long as was humanly possible.

By this time the Germans had succeeded in forcing the canal on both sides of the Company and there was a danger that one of Ervine-Andrews's forward positions would be overrun. Calling for volunteers from the Company headquarters to go forward with him, it was his intention to take up a position on the thatched roof of a barn.

There were seven or eight men with him at the time (Ervine-Andrews was not sure which figure was correct), but they volunteered to a man.

Climbing on to the roof of the barn, Ervine-Andrews discovered that the Bren gun they carried with them – an automatic weapon – was not working, so he had his soldiers load rifles and hand them up to him while efforts were made to repair the Bren. An excellent shot, he was able to inflict heavy casualties on the advancing German soldiers.

As a result, the Germans concentrated a devastating fire on the barn, sending mortar bombs and armour-piercing bullets through the roof, but before long the Bren gun was repaired. With this weapon, although hopelessly outnumbered, Ervine-Andrews was not only able to keep the Germans at bay but actually brought the whole German advance to a temporary halt.

For ten precious hours Ervine-Andrews held up the Germans, by which time half the men of his company had either been killed or wounded. With his ammunition once more almost exhausted, he gave the order for the survivors of B Company to make their way back to the lines, keeping only eight men with him at the barn until their last round was fired.

Despite the fact that he and his men were now virtually defenceless, Ervine-Andrews had no thought of surrendering to the Germans. Leading his men into the canal, he took them back towards Dunkirk, sometimes swimming, sometimes wading in water up to their necks, all the time being fired at by German

Harold Marcus Ervine-Andrews

soldiers who knew they were in the canal, but were never quite certain of their exact whereabouts.

Eventually, the small party came up against one of the British army's reserve companies and were able to climb out of the canal and make their way into Dunkirk.

It had been a desperate ten hours of fighting, but its success was incalculable to the success of the evacuation of the bulk of the British Expeditionary Force.

After the war, one of the German officers of the 18th Panzer Division – the unit opposing Ervine-Andrews and B Company – contacted the East Lancashire Regiment asking about the unit which had put up such a fierce resistance. He admitted that until then they had encountered so little serious opposition they had failed to carry out proper reconnaissance – and been badly mauled as a result.

It caused them to pause and consider their position, thus giving precious time to the British army and the gallant men in the fleet of small boats who crossed the Channel from Britain to evacuate them.

Had Ervine-Andrews and the men of B Company, 1st Battalion, the East Lancashire Regiment not made their stand, would history have been different? We will never know.

What we do know is that Ervine-Andrews and the survivors of his company, some 25 or 30 men, spent that night in a cellar in Dunkirk and were evacuated the following night in the destroyer, HMS *Shikari*.

Once back in England, Captain Ervine-Andrews was sent on attachment to the Royal Air Force in Cambridge, engaged on studying aerial photographs taken by reconnaissance aircraft of the French ports, where Hitler was assembling barges with the intention of invading England.

It was while he was here the news came through that he had been awarded the Victoria Cross – and he told an amusing story of that moment.

The squadron commander at Cambridge needed to go to London, and he invited Ervine-Andrews to go with him.

Whilst in London they found time to go out for dinner with the squadron commander's wife and her sister at a restaurant named 'Frascati's'. As was usual in war-time, the nine o'clock news was broadcast to the diners and, during the course of the news it was announced that the Victoria Cross had been awarded to a 'Captain Ervine-Andrews'.

Turning to the man himself, the squadron commander said, 'Did you hear that, Marcus? Is it a relative of yours?'

When Ervine-Andrews modestly admitted that *he* was the recipient of the world's most prestigious gallantry award, the effect in the restaurant was electrifying. Soon Champagne was arriving at the table from every quarter of the dining room.

Although the award of the Victoria Cross has to be the high point of any serviceman's career, Ervine-Andrews's life had been far from dull, even before the war. Commissioned into the East Lancashire Regiment in 1932, he served with the 2nd Battalion in Shanghai, Hong Kong and on the North West Frontier of India.

It was on the North West Frontier that he was 'mentioned in dispatches'. This occurred when he was a liaison officer with the RAF where, although not officially allowed to fly, he frequently flew with them on operations.

When the British were fighting Waziri tribesmen Ervine-Andrews was stationed at Dutta Hill Fort and, somehow, the Waziris got hold of an old Krupp field gun and began shelling the fort.

The tribesmen were not particularly good shots, but they did manage to hit the fort occasionally and were making something of a nuisance of themselves. Eventually, something had to be done about it and Ervine-Andrews led a party that sallied forth and captured the gun.

The following morning, the tribesmen sent a messenger into the fort with their abject apologies and said, 'Please, could they have their gun back.' If it was returned to them they promised they would go away and not bother the men in the fort any more.

As Ervine-Andrews himself said, it was 'a gentlemanly war'.

Later in World War II, after winning his Victoria Cross, Captain Ervine-Andrews was sent to Australia to train Royal Australian Air Force officers in direct air support of the army and here he established the RAAF School of Army Co-Operation, which eventually became the School of Direct Air Support.

He then went to New Guinea to arrange for a parachute company to be dropped on a Japanese-held island, then back to Britain in time for the invasion of Europe in June, 1944. After this he was sent to the Far East as Staff Air Liaison Officer to the Rear Admiral commanding the 21st Aircraft Carrier Squadron, a task force given responsibility for softening up Japanese airfields in the Singapore area.

In 1952, by now a Lieutenant Colonel, Marcus Ervine-Andrews left the army, eventually finding his way to a secluded house close to the small, South coast Cornish village of Gorran. Here he reared ducks, ornamental pheasants and other species of birds and lived a life far removed from those desperate 1940 days in France.

The medal won by Captain Marcus Ervine-Andrews is now on view, as he wished it to be, in the Museum of the Queen's Lancashire Regiment, in Preston, Lancashire.

A few months before his death on 30th March, 1995, this bravest of brave men declared he would never put the medal up for sale, explaining, 'I believe a medal of this sort belongs to the troops who won it and should give joy to descendants of chaps who were there and who actually helped to win it.'

Redvers Henry Buller 1839–1908

Lieutenant Colonel Redvers Buller (later General Sir Redvers Buller, VC, GCB, GCMG), saw more action during his lifetime than many of the soldiers who served in the armies of Queen Victoria. Born in Devon in December, 1839, at Downes House, Crediton, he was one of 11 children fathered by a man who had a long career in politics, first being Liberal M.P. for Exeter, and then representing North Devon from 1857 until his death in 1865, by which time Redvers was already a seasoned campaigner.

Educated at Harrow and Eton, it was always the intention of the young Buller to make his mark on the world in the army. Despite an injury which almost cost him a leg and left him with a limp, he obtained a commission in the 60th Rifles – later to become the King's Royal Rifle Corps – at the age of eighteen. It was a regiment that had played a prominent part in the Indian mutiny, two years before.

In 1860 as an Ensign in the Regiment's 2nd Battalion, he went to China where an Anglo-French force landed to enforce a trade treaty, grudgingly made and swiftly broken, by the Chinese. He was present at the storming of the Taku forts and took part in the occupation of Pekin – now Beijing.

Returning to England in 1862, later that year he was promoted to lieutenant and transferred to the 4th battalion serving in Canada, where he remained until 1869. Soon after he left the country, a rebellion broke out, led by Louis Riel, leader of a French-Indian tribe and Buller returned to Canada with a captain's rank. Here he attracted the attention of Lord Wolseley, who led a force against the rebels.

Although the expedition was involved in no fighting, Wolseley was impressed by Buller's skills in the Canadian backwoods. As a result, when Wolseley was putting together an expedition to West Africa, he asked for Buller to join the expedition.

Cutting short a course at the Staff College, Buller became Wolseley's Chief Intelligence Officer in the Ashanti wars and was wounded in action. Later he caught a serious fever and was sent home to England with the rank of Brevet Major and made a Companion of the Order of the Bath (CB).

In 1878, Buller became Special Service Officer to Lord Chelmsford, Commander-in-Chief, South Africa. Arriving there in March of that year, he was given command of the Frontier Light Horse Mounted Volunteers, who under his command became a highly efficient fighting force against the African tribes who were causing trouble in the Cape district.

Promoted to the rank of colonel, Buller and his Frontier Light Horse were with Lord Chelmsford's army which set off to attack the Zulu armies of King Cetshwayo. Advancing in three columns, Buller was in the left flank column led by Colonel Evelyn Wood, who had won a VC during the Indian Mutiny, in 1860.

Buller was involved in many skirmishes with the enemy until news reached Wood of the disaster which had overtaken the British army's central column. Attacked by an overwhelming Zulu army, the column had been annilihated, more than one thousand British soldiers being killed by a highly disciplined Zulu army. Colonel Wood promptly retreated to a strong position on a hill from which Buller and his Frontier Light Horse continued to harass the Zulus in their area.

Meanwhile, a section of the Zulu army attacked the tiny British garrison at Rorke's Drift, a place that was to become a legend in the annals of British army history when four thousand already victorious Zulu warriors descended upon the garrison of some one hundred and twenty men, forty of them being patients in the post's hospital.

Six times the vastly superior Zulu force launched determined attacks upon the small outpost – and six times they were repulsed, often in fierce hand-to-hand combat.

When the Zulu army retired at dawn, they left behind more than three hundred and fifty warriors lying dead on the sun-scorched veldt.

The Rorke's Drift defenders had suffered the loss of seventeen men killed and another ten wounded. This astounding victory brought the brave defenders a total of eleven VCs, more than would ever again be awarded for a single engagement.

It was now that the battle occurred for which the actions of Colonel Redvers Buller would earn him a Victoria Cross.

During a storm on the night of 27th March, 1879, Buller set out to mount an attack on the heavily defended mountain stronghold of Zulu Chief Mbilini. Before dawn on the 28th, Buller and his column reached the top of the mountain where they were met with fierce rifle fire from Zulu sentries.

In spite of the gunfire the column advanced steadily, driving the Zulus before them. Then, in the midst of the battle, the main Zulu army, 20,000 strong, was sighted, encouraging the Zulus in the mountain stronghold to mount a determined counter-attack.

In the circumstances, Buller had no choice but to give the order to men who by now were widely scattered on the mountain top, for a general retreat.

The order caused a certain amount of panic, but Buller ordered one of his

*Redvers
Henry
Buller*

officers, Lieutenant Everett, to form a rearguard with six men at the top of a steep pass down which he and his men would retreat and to assist any stragglers.

Under constant attack by the Zulus, Buller's main body of soldiers successfully withdrew. Then with his force providing covering fire, Buller went back to the aid of his rearguard, which was by now reduced to the lieutenant and two men.

Zulus swarmed all about the desperately fighting men and Lieutenant Everett's horse had been speared but Buller rode into the melee, rescued Everett and carried him to safety.

Then returning to the battle scene, Buller personally rescued a number of men, on more than one occasion carrying them to safety on his own horse. He then combed the area looking for any more stragglers who might still be struggling to reach safety.

The following day the Zulus attacked the main camp of the British soldiers who had formed a wagon laager and Buller led two squadrons of volunteer cavalry out against them.

Breaking the Zulu attack, he then pursued them, giving no quarter in an action that would later be heavily criticised in some British quarters as a 'slaughter'. Nevertheless, the victory won that day proved to be the turning point in the war against the Zulus and for his conduct Buller was awarded a Victoria Cross.

Few men have displayed greater bravery in close combat in the winning of this, the most prestigious of medals.

For five more months Buller led his men in fierce actions against the Zulus until, suffering from the effects of fatigue and exposure, he was sent back to England 'on medical grounds'.

On arrival in England Buller was feted as a hero and appointed an aide-de-camp to Queen Victoria – but he was not destined to spend the remainder of his service life enjoying society life in the shadow of the Queen of England.

In 1881 Buller returned to South Africa, playing a part in the war in which the Boers inflicted a humiliating defeating on the British. Back home once more, he married, only to be recalled from his honeymoon to travel to Egypt with Lord Wolseley as Chief Intelligence Officer.

This time, when he returned to England he was made a Knight Commander of the Order of St Michael and St George – but he did not remain at home for long. Soon he was in Africa once more, this time in command of the 1st Infantry Brigade in a campaign against Osman Digna, a slave dealer and Mahdi leader, active in the Red Sea area. During this campaign Buller so distinguished himself that he was promoted to the rank of major general.

He was later part of the expedition which failed to save General Gordon from death at Khartoum and he remained in Africa until October 1885, when he was recalled to London to become Deputy Adjutant General at the Horse Guards. Once again, he might have been expected to settle in a safe and not too onerous administrative post, but it was not to be. When the Boer War commenced he returned to the African continent and led an army that unsuccessfully tried to relieve Ladysmith, a failure for which he was criticised at the time and for which history has not always dealt with him kindly.

However, during his incredibly long and sometimes controversial career, his outstanding courage and fighting qualities were never in question and Lord Wolseley is on record as referring to him as the bravest man he had ever known. Always proud to be a Devon man until the time of his death in June 1908, General Sir Henry Redvers Buller, VC, GCB, GCMG, was a truly worthy recipient of the world's premier bravery award.

Reverend Theodore Bayley Hardy 1863–1918

One of the most highly decorated non-combatants in World War One, Reverend Theodore Hardy was possibly the most unassuming, brave and best loved chaplain ever to serve with the British army.

Theodore Bayley Hardy was born on 20th October, 1863, to George and Sarah Hardy, at Barnfield House, Southernhay, Exeter – a house that would later become the Exeter YMCA.

His father, a commercial traveller, died when Theodore was only three years old, leaving Sarah, now twice widowed, to cope with Theodore, his brother, Ernest, and a number of other sons from her first marriage.

To provide an income for her family she ran 'a preparatory school for young gentlemen' in the house and it was here Theodore was educated until at the age of about ten he was sent as a boarder to the City of London School.

Theodore greatly missed the family life he had known at Exeter and eagerly returned to his home city during the school holidays, until he enrolled as a student at London University, where he obtained a Bachelor of Arts degree in 1889, a year after he had married Grace Hastings, a Belfast girl.

After teaching in London for two years, during which time two children were born to the young couple, he became a housemaster at Nottingham High School. One of his students was DH Lawrence, who would one day became famous for such novels as *Lady Chatterley's Lover*, *The Rainbow*, and *Sons and Lovers*.

Having contemplated a career in the Church for many years, Theodore Hardy was ordained a deacon in the Church of England, in Southwell Minster, in 1898, and became a curate in the Nottinghamshire village of Burton Joyce, where he helped with the Sunday services, while continuing his teaching career.

A year later he was ordained a priest but remained at Burton Joyce for a further three years before accepting a curacy closer to his school. Then, in 1907, he became headmaster at Bentham Grammar School, close to Lancaster. It was a position he held until 1913, when Grace became seriously ill and was given only a short time to live. Resigning from the school, Hardy took up the post of vicar at Hutton Roof, in Westmorland.

Less than a year later, in June, 1914, Grace died and Theodore Hardy sought to submerge his grief in work until, in August of that year, war erupted in Europe, setting in motion events which would make this gentle and unassuming vicar from Westmorland the most famous chaplain in the British army.

Seven months after war was declared, Theodore's son, William, qualified as a doctor and, almost immediately joined the army in that capacity, being sent out to the Dardanelles within a matter of weeks.

Perhaps it was partly this that decided Reverend Theodore Hardy that he too should become involved in the war. Although now fifty-one years of age, he applied to become a military chaplain, only to be told there was a long waiting list of men much younger than himself.

Despite this, he applied time after time and, when he received the same reply, decided he would go to war as a volunteer stretcher bearer, taking and passing an ambulance course in order to further this aim.

Then, in mid-1916, a sudden shortage of chaplains occurred and Hardy was called for an interview. He was accepted and given the rank of captain, with the title of Temporary Chaplain, 4th Class.

At the end of August, 1916, Hardy was sent to France, where he became involved in the Somme offensive, during which British losses would total almost 420,000.

At first, he performed his duties in a base camp, but anxious to be sent to the front line where he believed he was most needed, in early December he succeeded in obtaining a posting to the 8th Battalion of the Lincolnshire Regiment with, soon afterwards, additional responsibility for the spiritual needs of the 8th Battalion of the Somerset Regiment, both regiments occupying positions in the Ypres area.

He arrived when the region was recording the hardest winter for some 35 years and infantrymen in the trenches were suffering severely from frostbite. Early in the New Year of 1917, the Lincolnshire Regiment and the Somersets took over a section of the line at Neuve Chapelle, where the trenches were hard frozen in bleak countryside. It was here Hardy decided he could best get to know the men he served by visiting them in the trenches at night and handing out sweets and cigarettes which he carried in a knapsack.

He soon became a familiar figure in the trenches during the night hours and also during the day too, whenever and wherever his services were needed.

In March, 1917, Hardy's regiment was withdrawn from the front-line trenches but instead of enjoying a well-earned rest with his men, Hardy, now fifty-three years of age, acquired a bicycle and set off on a ride of more than ninety kilometres to visit his much loved daughter, Elizabeth, who had arrived in France as a VAD Red Cross nurse, based in Dunkirk.

The respite from front-line duties was short-lived. By Easter Monday, 9th April, the Lincolns and Somersets were back in action. Called upon to go 'over the top', with bayonets fixed – their padre went with them. Almost immediately he became involved in helping to carry the wounded from the front to the dressing station and caring for the dying. During this action he worked for 36 hours without a break, but it was how he saw his duty. Wherever the fighting was fiercest, Theodore would be there to help the wounded and comfort the dying. More than once, he had to be ordered by the commanding officer to rest, but he found it hard.

During the fierce fighting in the Arras campaign the Lincolns lost more than half their men and Theodore Hardy was always wherever he felt he was most needed.

On 7th March, 1917, an incident occurred which was paraphrased in the London Gazette, as follows:

For conspicuous gallantry and devotion to duty in volunteering to go with a rescue party for some men who had been left stuck in the mud the previous night between the enemy's outpost line and our own. All the men except one were brought in. He then organised a party for the rescue of this man, and remained with them all night, though under fire at close range, which killed one of the party. With his left arm in splints, owing to a broken wrist, and under the worst weather conditions, he crawled out with patrols to within seventy yards of the enemy and remained with wounded men under heavy fire.

These were the circumstances for which Hardy was awarded the Distinguished Service Order and it was said that had the full facts been known at the time, he would have received the Victoria Cross.

Conditions in the Ypres area deteriorated rapidly in the months following the arrival of Theodore Hardy. By October, 1917, the whole area had been so badly churned up by shell-fire and poor weather that it would sometimes take as many as eight men to carry one stretcher. Despite this, Theodore did not go out with the occasional stretcher, but with every one. No mean feat for a man of fifty-three.

A light railway had been constructed on the front line and was used for bringing back the wounded. Hardy was travelling on this railway with two men of the Royal Army Medical Corps when a soldier from a nearby artillery battery called out that they had some severely wounded men. At this moment the Germans opened up a fearful bombardment, which seemed to destroy the whole surface of the earth. Despite this, Hardy and the medical men attended to the wounded men, disregarding their own safety. For this, he was awarded the Military Cross and the two medical orderlies the Military Medal.

By now, the war had become a nightmare for the men who were forced to man the trenches on the front line but, whenever his own battalions were relieved, Hardy would remain behind with the relieving battalion and at night, there would be a movement in the trenches and a soft voice would say, 'It's all right, boys, it's only me,' and Reverend Theodore Hardy would be there to talk to the soldiers of home, and share whatever cigarettes and sweets he had been able to bring with him. His words, 'It's only me' became so well known by the men that it was used as a title for an excellent biography of Theodore Hardy, written by David Raw.

In March, 1918, the German army, reinforced by men from the Russian front, where all resistance had collapsed, launched an attack in the area of the Somme that was intended to bring the war to a victorious close.

The 8th Lincolnshire Regiment, together with the 8th Somersets, were rushed from Ypres, arriving at the northern end of the Somme on 1st April. It was obvious that the Germans were massing for a final assault and so, on the night of 4/5th April, it was decided by the British generals that they would mount a pre-emptive strike.

They could hardly have chosen a worse night. Heavy rain was falling and the tanks detailed to support the attack were unable to advance. Nevertheless, at 5.30 in the morning, the men of the Lincolnshire Regiment were ordered to leave their trenches and go 'over the top'.

Almost immediately they were subjected to intense machine gun fire. Despite this, by 7.45am the enemy trenches had been secured, with the exception of two German strong points.

However it was not long before strong enemy reinforcements were brought up and the Lincolnshire Regiment was forced to withdraw to their original positions.

As the battalions re-grouped they realised that their padre, Theodore Hardy was missing and, as time went on, it was feared that he had become a casualty.

Then, as dusk approached, a small figure was seen coming towards them from a wood, which formed part of the German lines. It was Theodore Hardy. He had spent the whole day lying within yards of an enemy machine gun post, comforting a wounded man. Now he was asking for volunteers to return with him and recover the casualty.

A sergeant agreed to go with him and they crawled to where the wounded man lay. Although the casualty was too weak to stand, Hardy and the sergeant somehow managed to drag him back to the safety of a trench held by the Somersets.

Despite this harrowing ordeal, Hardy would not rest. Although continuous artillery, machine gun and trench-mortar fire caused many casualties, he moved quietly among the men, tending the wounded, completely regardless of his own safety.

For this and other similar exploits, Theodore Hardy was awarded the Victoria Cross. In the words of the Commander of the 37th Division, Major-General Bruce Williams, who gathered the statements of those who had witnessed this, and other similar exploits, 'The Chaplain really deserved it three times over.'

Reverend
Theodore
Bayley
Hardy

– but let the citation in the London Gazette of 11th July, 1918, tell the cold facts of Reverend Theodore Bayley Hardy's conduct for which he was awarded the Victoria Cross.

For most conspicuous bravery and devotion to duty on many occasions. Although over 50 years of age he has, by his fearlessness, devotion to men of his battalion and quiet, unobtrusive manner, won the respect and admiration of the whole division.

His marvellous energy and endurance would be remarkable even in a very much younger man and his valour and devotion are exemplified in the following incidents:

An infantry patrol had gone out to attack a previously located enemy post in the ruins of a village, the Reverend Theodore Bayley Hardy, CF, being then at company headquarters. Hearing firing, he followed the patrol and about 400 yards beyond our front line of posts, found an officer of the patrol dangerously wounded.

He remained with the officer until he was able to get assistance to bring him in. During this time there was a great deal of firing and an enemy patrol actually penetrated between the spot at which the officer was lying and our front line and captured three of our men.

On a second occasion when an enemy shell exploded in the middle of one of our posts, the Reverend TB Hardy at once made his way to the spot, despite shell and trench mortar fire which were going on at the time and set to work to extricate the buried men. He succeeded in getting out one man who had been completely buried. He then set to work to extricate a second man who was found to be dead.

During the whole of the time that he was digging out the men this chaplain was in great danger not only from shell fire but also because of the dangerous condition of the wall of the building which had been hit by the shell which buried the men.

On a third occasion he displayed the greatest devotion to duty when our infantry, after a successful attack, were gradually forced back to their starting trench.

After it was believed that all our men had withdrawn from the wood Chaplain Hardy came out of it and on reaching the advanced post, asked the men to help him to get in a wounded man. Accompanied by a sergeant, he made his way to the spot where the man lay, within ten yards of a pillbox which had been captured in the morning, but was subsequently recaptured and occupied by the enemy. The wounded man was too weak to stand, but between them the chaplain and the sergeant eventually succeeded in getting him to our lines.

Throughout the day the enemy's artillery, machine gun and trench mortar fire was continuous and caused many casualties.

Notwithstanding, this very gallant chaplain was soon moving quietly amongst the men and tending the wounded absolutely regardless of his personal safety.

The award was presented to Theodore Hardy on 9th August, 1918 by King George V at 3rd Army Headquarters, Frohen-le-Grande. The chaplain's daughter, Elizabeth, was a proud guest at the ceremony.

The King was so impressed with Hardy's record that, together with the Bishop of Carlisle, he attempted to save him from further risk. The King asked that he become one of his Chaplains in Ordinary and the Bishop offered him the vacant living of Caldbeck, in the Lakeland Fells, at twice the income of Hutton Roof, but Hardy felt he owed it to his parishioners to return to them when the war was over, and to his soldiers to remain with them until that happy day arrived.

On 10th October, 1918, the two battalions to which Theodore Hardy was attached were ordered to cross the River Selle in a general advance against the Germans. In the darkness, a small figure crossed to join them and the familiar words were heard, 'It's only me, boys.'

Soon afterwards a German machine gun opened fire and Hardy was shot through the thigh. Braving the machine gun fire, stretcher bearers reached him and when they found him, he apologised to them, saying, 'I'm sorry to give you all this trouble boys, when you are urgently needed elsewhere.' He was evacuated by train to the No 2 Red Cross Hospital at Rouen, a hundred miles away and his daughter, Elizabeth, was sent for.

A week later, on 18th October, 1918 Reverend Theodore Hardy, VC, DSO, MC, died, two days before his 55th birthday and this exceptionally brave and Christian man was buried in the St Sever Military Cemetery at Rouen, France, deeply mourned by men he so ably served in their time of need.

The war ended three weeks later.

Elizabeth, the daughter of this remarkable man never married and, after becoming Headmistress of a Girl's Secondary School in Rangoon, narrowly evaded capture by the Japanese when escaping through Burma in World War II. After a period as Head of a School in Bangalore, she retired to Cornwall.

The Indian Mutiny 1857
– and 4 VCs for the 32nd(Cornwall) Regiment

The Duke of Cornwall Light Infantry Museum at The Keep, Bodmin, in the heart of Cornwall, displays with pride the record of a regiment whose history spans more than 300 years. In March, 1702, Queen Anne decreed that a Regiment of Fox's Marines be raised and, in that first year they secured a notable victory against the Spanish in Vigo Bay, taking treasure worth more than a million pounds.

Two years later Fox's Marines gained their first official battle honour when they took part in the storming of Gibraltar. They were reformed in 1715 as the 32nd Regiment, which in 1782 became the 32nd (Cornwall) Regiment.

In 1881, the 32nd merged with the 46th (South Devonshire) Regiment (raised in 1748), to become the 1st and 2nd Battalions of the Duke of Cornwall's Light Infantry, with their headquarters and depot in Bodmin.

Before this occurred, the 32nd had written a glorious chapter in the regiment's history when no fewer that four Victoria Crosses were awarded to its soldiers serving at Lucknow during the Indian Mutiny of 1857.

The reasons for the 'mutiny' are many, varied and contradictory. One of the oft-quoted causes was the issue of a new type of cartridge which, it was rumoured, was soaked in cow and pork fat, something abhorrent to the Sepoys' religion.

But this was perhaps no more than a catalyst for a whole series of grievances, fuelled by the indifference or downright arrogance of some British officers towards the native troops under their command.

Such indifference was foolhardy in the extreme. India had a population of some 150 million with a standing army of 300,000 men, of whom less than 5% were European. True, about 23,000 soldiers of the British army were also in the country, but most were engaged in protecting the frontiers of the recently annexed province of Punjab against warlike tribesmen from Afghanistan.

Reports and rumours of an impending uprising of Indian soldiers against their European overlords had been circulating for some time, and there had been a number of comparatively minor incidents, but those in a position to do something about it refused to believe there was anything to be feared from the native soldiers whom, they declared, would never harm those who had taken their country from them. As a result, when the mutiny erupted with frightening suddenness and violence, it was some time before its true seriousness was fully appreciated.

Before listing the individual feats of gallantry, it might prove helpful to describe the events which led to the soldiers of the besieged 32nd Regiment withstanding 140 days of constant attack in the British Residency of Lucknow, during which time they lost 15 officers and 364 other ranks killed, in addition to 11 officers and 198 men wounded. Scores of men, together with their women and children, also succumbed to sickness and disease in the appalling conditions prevailing within the walls of the Residency.

In addition to the casualties sustained at Lucknow, the regiment also lost three officers, 82 other ranks, 47 women and 55 children. They were among the hundreds of men, women and children butchered by mutineers in an act of treachery at the nearby outpost of Cawnpore, on the western bank of the sacred River Ganges.

At Cawnpore, the officer in charge was 67 year-old Major-General Sir Hugh Massy Wheeler who had spent most of his life in India, was married to an Indian woman and spoke the language of the Indian troops under his command.

In May, 1857, when sporadic trouble was breaking out in other parts of the country, Wheeler sent a message to the Governor-General of India assuring him that all was well at Cawnpore and that the troubles the country was experiencing would be over within a few days.

Not sharing his confidence, officers under his command urged Sir Hugh to take up a defensive position within the sturdily built magazine building, but their suggestion was dismissed out of hand. Should there be any trouble, which he scornfully dismissed, Sir Hugh declared it would be sufficient for anyone who felt threatened to make for the barracks entrenchment, situated in an exposed position on the plain to the east of the city. Because of his convictions, he did not feel it necessary to stock the barracks with provisions for more than twenty-five days.

On the night of 5th June, despite Sir Hugh's misguided complacency, mutiny broke out in Cawnpore among his Indian regiments and before long the barracks entrenchment was under attack. Inside were some two hundred European soldiers – many of them sick – a hundred European officers from the native regiments, about the same number of civilians and four hundred women and children.

The siege lasted until almost the end of June, by which time conditions within the entrenchment were indescribable and every day brought new casualties. In the meantime, the mutineers were being reinforced by men from the surrounding countryside who saw this as an opportunity to rid their country of the European occupiers.

Eventually, Nana Sahib, the Indian leader of the mutineers, once a staunch

The Residency, Lucknow shortly after the end of the siege

friend of the British, offered terms for the surrender of those within the entrenchment. They would be allowed to leave their defensive position and provided with boats to take them downriver to Allahabad.

Sir Hugh accepted Nana Sahib's conditions and, on 27th June, 1857, with the women, children and wounded riding on elephants and in bullock carts, the exhausted and dispirited survivors left the entrenchment and made their way to the river, watched by the residents of Cawnpore who had come from their homes in their hundreds to witness the defeated British garrison leave.

At the river, the men, women and children had begun boarding the boats when suddenly, from vantage points on both sides of the river, the mutineers who were waiting in a well planned ambush, opened fire with small arms and artillery.

General Wheeler was cut down by a sword thrust in the slaughter that continued until there was no one left capable of putting up any resistance. All the men and older boys were killed and about a hundred and twenty five women and children captured. These were later joined by a number of officers' wives who had been taken elsewhere in the area.

It is not the purpose of this book to give details of atrocities committed by both sides during the months of the mutiny, but the women and children captured by Nana Sahib and his army suffered appallingly before, on 15th July, with a relief force under General Havelock nearing the house in which they were crammed, more than two hundred British women and children were slaughtered and their bodies tossed into a well in the garden.

Such was the fate of the men and women of the Cawnpore garrison, which included men, women and children belonging to the 32nd (Cornwall) Regiment. There were many deeds of great bravery during their ordeal, worthy of the highest honour, but their stories would come out only piecemeal from Indians who witnessed them. No Europeans survived to record their story.

Meanwhile, at Lucknow, where the 32nd was the only European regiment in the area, there were a number of minor incidents before full-scale mutiny erupted on the night of 30th May, and many of the outlying families frantically sought refuge in the Lucknow British Residency building. Among them were civilians of the Indian Civil Service who were immediately given weapon training by the NCOs of the 32nd Regiment.

For the whole of the month of June refugees streamed into Lucknow, bringing with them harrowing stories of what they had suffered at the hands of Indian mutineers and their supporters, yet Lucknow itself was not immediately attacked.

Then the official occupant of the Residency, Sir Henry Lawrence, heard that a rebel force was advancing to attack Lucknow, and he took out a force of some 600 men, including soldiers of the 32nd to oppose them.

There were many more Indian mutineers than was realised and they were led by a skilful commander, one Barkat Ahmad, who lured Lawrence's men into a trap, killing many of them.

The survivors straggled back to Lucknow, hotly pursued by the mutineers. As the last of the men of the 32nd, stumbled inside the Residency, the gates were swung closed and the siege of Lucknow had begun.

Before the mutiny erupted, Sir Henry Lawrence had been given absolute power over Lucknow and the surrounding area – and he used it well. The Residency was fortified and supplies brought in that would ensure survival for those occupants who were not carried away by disease or enemy action during the harrowing siege that followed.

A relief column under General Sir Henry Havelock fought its way into Lucknow on 25th September, supplying desperately needed reinforcements for the rapidly dwindling occupants of the Residency, but it was not in sufficient force to end the siege which lasted for 140 horrendous days. When it began the Residency held some 2,000 people, of whom 237 were women, and 260 children. By the end, some two-thirds of these had died and an epic chapter had been written in the history of the 32nd Regiment.

The stories of the four members of the 32nd (Cornwall) Regiment who were awarded VCs follow.

William Oxenham 1821–1874

Born in Tiverton, Devon on 15th October, 1821, William Oxenham was a young married man with a daughter when he enlisted in the 32nd Regiment in April 1842. In May, 1846, he sailed to India with the regiment and fought in the Sikh War of 1848-49.

The bulk of the 32nd was stationed at Lucknow when the mutiny erupted and the Residency besieged. A number of European houses were being used as outposts at this time and one was a house occupied by a Bengal Civil Servant, named Capper. On 30th June, 1857, the outpost was considered to be of such importance that the defenders were ordered to hold it at all costs.

Unfortunately, the mutineers also recognised its importance and brought their artillery to bear on the building. One of their shots brought down the verandah, burying Capper beneath six feet of rubble.

One of the British officers, Captain Anderson, called for volunteers to try to rescue the Bengal civil servant. Corporal Oxenham volunteered immediately and accompanied by a Frenchman, an Italian and two more Englishmen went out to extricate the Bengal Civil Servant.

Meanwhile, the enemy continued to bombard the building and the would-be rescuers were forced to lie on their stomachs as they attacked the rubble in an effort to locate Capper.

Eventually, he was found alive and the rubble cleared from most of his body, but his legs remained trapped. To stand up in order to remove the debris from the trapped man's legs was to invite almost certain death. Despite this, Oxenham dashed around to the exposed side of the pile of rubble and, working frantically under fire from the mutineers, eventually succeeded in freeing Capper and the unfortunate civil servant was hauled clear.

The rescue took three-quarters of an hour during which time the rescuers were under constant cannon and musket fire from the mutineers. They all showed exceptional bravery but, for his almost suicidal effort in freeing Capper's legs, Corporal Oxenham would receive the Victoria Cross, the first of four awarded to men of the 32nd (Cornwall) Regiment.

Oxenham was seriously wounded before Lucknow was relieved, but he had recovered by the time the regiment returned to England in 1859, having been away from its home country for thirteen years. During this time, Oxenham's wife had

William Oxenham

died, although the details of her death are not known.

In February, 1860, he married Caroline Pulman, daughter of a Halberton blacksmith, at St Edmund's Church, Exeter, and it was in this city that he died of meningitis on 29th December, 1874, at the age of fifty-three.

At the time of his death, Oxenham's estate totalled less than twenty pounds and his wife could not afford a memorial for him. It was not until 1993 that a headstone was raised in the Dissenter's section of the Exeter's Higher Cemetery for this brave soldier.

William Dowling 1825–1887

An Irishman, William Dowling was born at Thomastown, County Kilkenny in about 1825 and enlisted in the 32nd Regiment in 1845, when it was stationed in Ireland. A year later the regiment sailed for India and Dowling would serve there for the next fourteen years, during which time he earned a reputation as one of the most undisciplined soldiers in the regiment – unless there was a battle to be fought, when he could be found where the fighting was fiercest.

The 32nd fought in a great many battles during the years it served in India, and Dowling seemed to be present at most of them. In the Sikh wars he was with the 32nd when it won Battle Honours at Mooltan, Gujerat and Punjab, but the most desperate battle of all was still to come – at Lucknow. It was here, during the siege, that Dowling was to play a great part in what would be one of the one of the most glorious episodes in the Regiment's long history.

From being one of the 32nd's most rebellious soldiers, Dowling began to display exceptional courage and leadership and he was promoted corporal.

Conditions within the Lucknow Residency were dire. Nowhere was safe from the mutineers' musketry and cannon fire, and cholera and a lack of milk for the babies meant there were many deaths and wounded among the ever-dwindling occupants.

When the besiegers brought heavy cannon close to the residency, they caused even more casualties and it was believed they would soon break down the already battered and broken walls.

The guns were well dug in and guarded, and withering covering fire could be brought to bear should an attempt be made to spike the guns. 'Spiking' involved a man, or men, braving enemy bullets as they dashed from the fort to the gun pit, overpowering the mutineers manning the gun, then hammering an iron spike into the touch hole of the cannon and breaking it off flush with the barrel so it could not be removed.

Such an attempt was considered suicidal, yet Dowling made just such a sortie not once, or even twice, but on three occasions. Let the subsequent citation take up the story:

For distinguished gallantry on 4 July 1857, in going out with two other men, since dead, and spiking two of the enemy guns.

Also for distinguished gallantry, on the 9th of the same month, in going out again with three men, since dead, to spike one of the enemy guns. He had to retire, the spike being too small, but was exposed to the same danger.

Also, for distinguished bravery, on the 27th September, 1857, in spiking an 18 pounder gun during a sortie, he being at the same time under a most heavy fire.

His rebellious past service now well and truly behind him, Dowling was promoted sergeant and received the Victoria Cross from Queen Victoria at a ceremony held at Windsor Castle on 4th January 1860.

Shortly afterwards, William Dowling, VC was pensioned from the army and, after marrying, went to live in Kirkdale, in Liverpool, where he was employed as a customs officer by HM Customs and Excise. He died in Stanley hospital on 17th February, 1887.

The Victoria Cross

Samuel Hill Lawrence 1831–1868

Samuel Hill Lawrence was born in Cork, Ireland, on the 22nd of January, 1831, and received a commission as ensign in the 32nd Regiment in December, 1847, at the age of sixteen.

Joining the regiment in India in 1847, he was present at many of the battles in which the 32nd was engaged during its long tour of duty in that country and in 1850 was sufficiently experienced for there to be no barrier put in his way when he purchased a promotion to lieutenant.

He was in the Residency at Lucknow when it was besieged by mutineers and suffered with the other occupants – but not without taking every opportunity to hit back at those surrounding the small and motley garrison.

One of the great fears of those inside the Residency was that mutineer miners might drive a tunnel beneath the compound and set off an explosion that would demolish a section of the protective wall, allowing the mutineers to storm and occupy the Residency.

A constant listening watch was kept in an attempt to foil such an attempt, but the danger was ever present and, early in July suspicion was aroused that the mutineers were digging a tunnel from a building not very far from the Residency walls and a party led by Lieutenant Lawrence sallied forth from the beleagured garrison to examine the house.

Lawrence was an officer who led by example and he was the first to climb the ladder placed against a window of the house. His pistol was knocked from his hand by one of the defending mutineers, but Lawrence was not deterred. Despite the fierce opposition met with inside the house, he succeeded in establishing that there was no tunnel and, his mission accomplished, Lawrence succeeded in returning to the safety of the Residency with his surviving men.

In September, when the Residency had been under siege for almost three months, reinforcements reached Lucknow, but not in sufficient numbers to raise the siege and fierce fighting was still going on. The mutineers' artillery in particular was causing great distress to those inside the Residency compound and, on 26th September, Lieutenant Lawrence, at the head of a party of soldiers charged out of the compound and in a daring and fierce fought sortie captured a 9-pounder gun that had been causing particular distress to those in the Lucknow Residency.

It eased the immediate problem, but it was not until 17th November, that

Sir Colin Campbell and his Highlanders reached Lucknow with a strong relieving force and brought the desperate siege to an end.

Lieutenant (later Major) Samuel Hill Lawrence became the third man of the 32nd Regiment to win the Victoria Cross in what was known at the time as the 'Indian Mutiny'.

He died at the early age of 37 in Montevideo, Uruguay on 17th June 1868.

Samuel Hill Lawrence

Henry George Gore-Brown 1830–1912

The fourth member of the 32nd Regiment to win a Victoria Cross at Lucknow was, like Dowling and Lawrence, an Irishman. Born at Newtown, Roscommon on 30th September, 1830, he came from a noble family, one of his ancestors being the 1st Earl of Altamont. Another was Admiral Sir Richard Hughes, who had Horatio Nelson serving as one of his captains in 1786.

During the siege, one of the houses close to the Residency building became a danger to the beleaguered defenders when the mutineers succeeded in mining a section of the Residency defensive palisade and used the house as a base for their activities.

It was decided that the house should be blown up, but the British Engineers knew this would be impossible unless two rebel artillery pieces could be put out of action. Captain Gore-Browne was detailed to lead a party of 50 men of the 32nd Regiment in carrying out this highly dangerous task.

The guns were protected by a high palisade with sliding shutters sealing off the gun embrasures and were defended by a great many of the enemy. Despite the odds against them, Gore-Browne and his men reached the gun position and, being an officer accustomed to leading his men into battle, it was Gore-Browne who succeeded in removing the shutters and jumping into the battery to successfully spike the guns.

Some idea of the sheer ferocity of the fighting that went on about Gore-Browne as he carried out his work can be gained by the knowledge that when the small party fought its way back to the Residency, some 100 rebels were left lying dead behind them.

The citation for Gore-Browne's Victoria Cross is a masterly example of understatement. It reads,

On 21 August 1857 at Lucknow, India, during the Siege of the Residency, Captain Browne led a sortie for the purpose of spiking two heavy guns which were doing considerable damage to the defences. The guns were protected by high palisades, the embrasures being closed with sliding shutters. On reaching the battery, Captain Browne removed the shutters, jumped into the battery and spiked the guns. It is supposed that about 100 of the enemy were killed in this operation.

Captain Gore-Browne remained with the 32nd Regiment, attaining the rank of colonel before he retired to the Isle of Wight to become one of its most respected citizens. A personal friend of Queen Victoria, who had a home on the island, he became a Justice of the Peace, and was made Deputy Governor of the Isle of Wight.

It was here at Shanklin that he died on 15 November 1912, a brave man who had brought honour to his family and to the regiment he served so well.

The four Victoria Crosses won by the soldiers of the 32nd Regiment at Lucknow are all on display together with four other VCs to which the Regiment has a claim, at the DCLI Regimental Museum in the Keep, in Bodmin, Cornwall, once the depot of the Duke of Cornwall's Light Infantry.

Henry George Gore-Browne

John Prettyjohn 1823–1887

One of the first Victoria Crosses ever awarded went to Corporal John Prettyjohn of the Royal Marines Light Infantry. Indeed, the action for which he was awarded the medal took place on 5th November 1854, more than year before the Victoria Cross was instituted by Royal Warrant on 29 January, 1856.

The Battle of Inkerman occurred less than a fortnight after the *Charge of the Light Brigade* – immortalised in Tennyson's poetry – and it was fought in a particularly chaotic manner.

The British and French were besieging Sebastopol, but when the Russian defenders were reinforced to such an extent that they greatly out-numbered their enemies, the Russian commanders decided they would attempt to break the siege.

The morning on which they launched their offensive turned out to be so foggy that an experienced commander-in-chief would have called off the proposed attack because of the difficulty in co-ordinating the troops involved. But the Russian commanders were no more effective than their British and French counterparts. The orders had been given and no one in authority had the courage to countermand them.

The result was one of the most disjointed battles of a war which excelled in confusion. Orders on both sides were given and almost immediately countermanded. What was intended to be a planned battle disintegrated into a series of incredibly fierce skirmishes in which it was not always clear who was friend, and who was foe.

In the front line of the besieging army at the time were some three hundred men of the Royal Marines Light Infantry, commanded by Captain WF Hopkins. They were under almost constant attack, but when word came in that enemy snipers were occupying caves on a nearby hill, a small party of marines, led by Sergeant Richards, was sent to flush them out. In the party was Corporal John Prettyjohn, a Devon man.

The marines carried out their task well, but in so doing came close to exhausting their ammunition. Then through the mist they saw a party of Russian soldiers advancing up the hill towards them, in single file.

Greatly outnumbered and short of ammunition, Prettyjohn instructed the marines to collect as many rocks as they could. This they did. Then, taking up an advanced position, the marines laid low to await the arrival of the Russians.

John Prettyjohn

When they loomed up out of the mist in front of him, Corporal Prettyjohn succeeded in shooting four of them. Then, picking up the next Russian in the line and, using a West Country wrestling throw, he heaved him at the line of Russian soldiers climbing the hill in his wake. When they tumbled down in confused surprise, the Royal Marines pelted them with rocks and, as they wavered, fired the last of their ammunition at them.

It was enough. The Russians fled, leaving Prettyjohn and his Marine colleagues victorious. For this audacious feat, John Prettyjohn was awarded one of the first ever Victoria Crosses and went on to become a colour sergeant, seeing more action in the China Wars a few years later.

Prettyjohn was born at Dean Prior, Ashburton, Devon on 11th June, 1823 and joined the Royal Marines at Stonehouse Barracks, Devonport in June, 1844, after working as a labourer. He served in the Royal Marines for twenty-one years, retiring on pension in June 1865. During his service years, Prettyjohn married and had two daughters, one of whom did not die until 1960, at the age of ninety-five.

John Prettyjohn, VC died in Manchester on 20 January 1887 and is buried there.

Peter Scawen Watkinson Roberts 1917–1979

True bravery has many guises. It perhaps manifests itself most often in the heat of battle, when it is not always possible to stand back and assess the possible outcome of one's actions. This is not to belittle in any way the sheer courage of such deeds, when, in many circumstances, no criticism would be made for doing nothing at all.

But there is another kind of courage, when there is time to assess the implications of taking a certain course of action, knowing full well that should it not succeed, death is inevitable.

Such a decision was made by two men, Lieutenant Peter Scawen Watkinson Roberts and Petty Officer Thomas William Gould, serving on board HM Submarine *Thrasher*, on 17th February, 1942, off the north coast of Crete.

The day before, the submarine had torpedoed and sunk an enemy supply ship, which was being escorted by a number of anti-submarine vessels supported by aircraft.

As a result, the German aircraft and surface vessels made a determined attempt to destroy *Thrasher* in a series of sustained attacks which lasted until *Thrasher* made good its escape, aided by darkness, only surfacing when it was necessary to recharge the submarine's batteries.

In the early hours of the 17th February, *Thrasher* altered course and with a beam swell, began to roll uncomfortably. It was now that some unusual noises were heard from the deck of the submarine, as though a heavy object was rolling about between the hull and the casing of the submarine, just forward of the 4-inch gun mounting.

When investigations were carried out it was discovered that the moving object was an unexploded enemy bomb trapped inside the deck casing, a metal structure which created a narrow decking on the submarine's hull. At any moment it was likely that the movement of the submarine would cause the bomb to explode.

Lieutenant Roberts – the vessel's first lieutenant, and PO Gould, the second coxswain, volunteered to go on deck and attempt to remove the highly dangerous object. It was a desperately risky operation. Should the motion of the sea cause the bomb to roll off the casing and drop onto the tanks on either side of the submarine, the vessel and its crew were doomed.

The first thing to do was to prevent the unacceptable movement of the bomb and this was achieved in the simplest possible manner – albeit it a dangerous one. PO Gould held the bomb still while Lieutenant Roberts fetched a potato sack, which was placed about the bomb and held in place by a length of rope.

Because of its weight it was impossible to throw the bomb clear of the submarine's tanks and so it was necessary for the two men to manhandle the bomb, which weighed about a hundred pounds, to the bows of the submarine. No mean feat in the heavy swell being experienced by the vessel.

Here while *Thrasher* went full astern, the bomb was dropped overboard and the two men breathed a sigh of relief that was to be frighteningly short-lived.

As they made their way back to the submarine's conning tower along the casing they discovered an ominous hole. Investigating, they discovered a *second* unexploded bomb. Trapped inside the casing it was resting on top of the hull. If this bomb exploded it would blow a hole in the submarine that would send it to the bottom of the sea within a matter of minutes!

It was immediately apparent that the bomb could not be manhandled to safety through the hole it had made in the casing. It could only extracted through a trapdoor in the metal casing, about six metres away. Reaching a swift decision, the two men lowered themselves through the trapdoor into a space that was little more than half-a metre high, between the casing and the hull of the submarine.

Wriggling on their stomachs, they reached the spot where the bomb was wedged. It was an extremely dangerous situation for more than one reason. If the bomb exploded they and the submarine would plunge to the bottom of the sea. There was also a very real risk that while they worked the enemy would find *Thrasher* on the surface. The submarine was off an enemy coast and the Germans knew they were in the vicinity. If a ship or aircraft located them, the captain of the submarine would have no alternative but to dive – and both men inside the casing would drown.

Roberts and Gould were aware of this, but they tried not to think of it. Reaching the bomb, Gould succeeded in cradling the bomb in his arms. Then, lying on his back, he was pulled along the cramped casing towards the trapdoor by Roberts.

This part of the operation took a long forty minutes but, finally, the hazardous operation was completed and the two men were able to wrap the bomb in the sack, carry it forward and drop it over the bows of the submarine, as they had done with the first German bomb.

Both men were awarded the Victoria Cross on 9th June, 1942, and few awards can have been more deserving.

Peter Scawen Watkinson Roberts was born on 28th July 1917 in Chesham Bois, Buckinghamshire, and went to King's School in Canterbury before joining

*Peter Scawen
Watkinson Roberts*

the Navy in 1935. After a period on board the training ship *Frobisher*, he served on surface vessels before joining the submarine service soon after the outbreak of war in 1939 and being drafted to *Thrasher* in January 1941, as its first lieutenant.

Prior to receiving the Victoria Cross, Roberts had been recommended for the Distinguished Service Cross, an award that was announced after he received the VC.

In 1942 Lieutenant Roberts, VC, DSC, left the submarine service and saw active service in the Far East. Later, he served on board the frigate *Cardigan Bay* during the Korean War before retiring from the Royal Navy in 1962.

In February, 1940, Roberts had married Brigid Lethbridge at Plymouth. They had a son and a daughter and, upon his retirement, lived in Newton Ferrers, Devon, until the death of this very courageous naval officer on 8th December, 1979.

Richard Douglas Sandford 1891–1919

It was perhaps appropriate that one of the most audacious seaborne assaults carried out against the Germans in World War One, should take place on St George's Day, 23rd April, 1918. The attack was made simultaneously at Zeebrugge, and Ostend, ports in Belgium some 20 kilometres apart, which provided access to the sea from the vital naval base the Germans had created at Bruges.

The base provided a safe haven for destroyers, torpedo boats and, in particular, U-boats, the submarine arm of the German navy which had wreaked such havoc with British ships that at one time it was feared it might alter the course of the war.

The object of the raid was to seal off Bruges. Although by no means an unqualified success in this respect, it gave a much needed boost to British morale and shook German confidence in the invulnerability of their harbour defences. It also witnessed some incredible acts of bravery by sailors and Royal Marines, no fewer than 8 VCs being awarded to those who landed at Zeebrugge, and 3 to those at Ostend. However, the percentage of men killed and wounded was very high indeed.

Lieutenant Richard Sandford was one the men raiding Zeebrugge. Here, the entrance to the canal giving access to Bruges was protected by a curving mole, about two-and-a-half kilometres long and bristling with guns of all sizes.

The main assault vessel carrying the raiding party was an 1899 cruiser, *Vindictive*, on one side of which ramps had been fitted. These would be dropped when the vessel came alongside the mole, allowing the assault party to land en masse and take the gun positions. At the same time, a number of block ships would be positioned and sunk in the entrance of the canal, thus sealing off the main waterway leading to Bruges.

On the night of 22nd/23rd April, with no moon and under the cover of a smoke screen it was hoped *Vindictive* would reach the mole without being seen until the last moment.

It was not to be.

The assault cruiser was sighted when it was still some distance from the mole and the Germans, backed up by the guns of two destroyers moored on the far side of the mole, opened a murderous barrage on the raiders. Shells of all sizes punched holes in *Vindictive's* superstructure and the commanding officers of both the Royal Marines and the naval assault parties were both killed outright, many other officers being also killed or wounded.

The sailors manning *Vindictive's* guns also suffered very heavy casualties and, perhaps far more serious, all except two of the landing ramps were destroyed, with the result that when the cruiser eventually got alongside the mole, the German gunners could concentrate on these as the men desperately scrambled ashore.

Many deeds of incredible valour were performed by the men on board *Vindictive*, but Lieutenant Sandford was not with this main body. A submarine officer, he was in command of one of two obsolete British submarines, both packed with explosives, being towed to Zeebrugge to be positioned against a rail and road viaduct which connected the mole to the shore.

Half-a-kilometre in length, destruction of the viaduct would prevent the Germans from reinforcing their forces on the mole and also render it less effective in the defence of Zeebrugge.

Unfortunately, on passage the tow broke on the second submarine and Lieutenant Sandford and his crew, comprised of another officer and four men, were left to carry out the task as best they could on their own.

As the submarine approached the scene of the action and cast off to proceed under its own power, the vessel was illuminated by German star-shells and searchlights, but for some unknown reason was not immediately fired upon.

The submarine had been specially adapted so that the men on board could set a course for the viaduct and abandon their vessel, using a small motor launch to escape while the submarine headed for its target.

Perhaps because the destruction of the viaduct was now entirely in his hands, Sandford decided not to make use of the special equipment. Instead, bringing the crew up on deck, he ran in beneath the viaduct at all the speed of which the old submarine was capable, hitting with such an impact that part of the submarine protruded from the far side and the conning tower was wedged in the framework of steel girders beneath the viaduct.

Ordering the crew into the motor launch, Sandford set the fuses, which had a twelve minute delay, before joining the others. By now the Germans had realised what was happening and opened fire from the viaduct upon the submariners. Sandford and two of his crew were wounded – and the engine of the launch would not start!

Getting out paddles, they began to row for their lives, aware that the submarine would soon explode. Sandford was wounded again, as were the two men who were paddling and they had not got far away when the submarine exploded – and with it the viaduct. Richard Douglas Sandford's part in the raid, at least, had been a total success.

*Richard Douglas
Sandford*

Shortly afterwards, Sandford and his crew were picked up by one of the Royal Navy's escort boats and taken out to the destroyer, *Phoebe*.

Richard Sandford spent a full three months in hospital recovering from his wounds, but on 31st July, 1918, was fit enough to join other Zeebrugge heroes and receive his Victoria Cross from King George V.

It was an honour that, sadly, he would not enjoy for long. Born at Exmouth, in Devon, on 11th May, 1891, the seventh son of Ernest Grey Sandford, Archdeacon of Exeter, Lieutenant Richard Douglas Sandford, VC, died of typhoid in Cleveland Hospital, Grangetown, Yorkshire on 23rd November, 1918, less than a fortnight after the Armistice was signed. He is buried nearby, in Eston cemetery.

Arthur Leyland Harrison 1886–1918

Details of the Zeebrugge raid have already been given and there can be no doubt that the fighting during the dark hours of St George's Day, 1918, was as desperate as anything experienced during this bitterly fought war. Before HMS *Vindictive* even reached its objective the ship had been pounded at close range by German guns of various calibres, killing the commanding officers of the naval assault force and the Royal Marines.

Lieutenant Commander Harrison, a member of the Royal Navy storming party, took command of the naval assault force even though he had himself been wounded by a shell splinter which broke his jaw and rendered him temporarily unconscious.

When he came round, and although in great pain, he placed himself at the head of his men and led them in a desperate attack on the German batteries, aware that any delay in silencing the enemy guns was likely to jeopardise the success of the whole operation. Sadly, every man of his party was either killed or wounded.

Among those killed was Harrison himself. He died leading his men into action, although already severely wounded and aware that he faced almost certain death. For the extreme bravery he showed in this heroic action Lieutenant Commander Harrison was awarded a posthumous Victoria Cross which was presented to his widow by King George V in a ceremony at Buckingham Palace on 17th May, 1919.

Harrison was born at Torquay in Devon on 3rd February, 1886, the son of a lieutenant colonel in the Royal Fusiliers and joined the Royal Navy in September, 1902. After commanding a torpedo boat, he transferred to HMS *Lion*, flagship of Admiral Beatty and was 'mentioned in despatches' during the battle of Jutland.

A superb athlete, Harrison played rugby football at the highest level, gaining two International caps playing for England in 1913-1914 and his charge against the guns of the German army at Zeebrugge has been likened to the charge of a determined forward in a high-class rugby football match.

Lieutenant Commander Arthur Leyland Harrison, VC, was a sailor of whom the seafaring county of Devon can be justly proud.

Arthur Leyland Harrison

James Power Carne 1906–1986

The Korean War is often referred to as the 'Forgotten War', and perhaps it is for many people today, but it is not forgotten by those who fought there, nor will they forget the many brave men who died fighting under the banner of the United Nations in this remote corner of Asia.

The war in Korea also had quite as many heroes as any other conflict in which British servicemen were involved, and the West Country was well represented. One of the most revered heroes of the war was James Power Carne, who was born in Falmouth, Cornwall, on 11th April, 1906, and who joined the Gloucestershire Regiment in 1925.

He quickly made his mark in the regiment. An excellent shot, he also became a member of both the rugby football fifteen and the athletics team. After serving for five years as a subaltern, Lieutenant Carne was seconded to the King's African Rifles, remaining with them in East Africa until 1936.

Returning to the 28th battalion of his regiment as adjutant, he was responsible for embarking the battalion for Burma in December, 1938, but when war broke out less than a year later, Captain Carne was recalled to become a Company commander in the 7th Battalion.

He then held a number of posts in the regiment until, in the second half of the war he was appointed to command the 26th Battalion of the King's African Rifles in the Burma campaign, during which he was 'mentioned in despatches.'

When the war ended he remained with the King's African Rifles in British Somaliland until he was recalled to command the 5th Battalion of the Gloucestershire Regiment.

Then, in the summer of 1950, the Korean War erupted and James Carne, by now Lieutenant Colonel in command of the 1st Battalion, Gloucestershire Regiment, took his men to war once again.

Many of the battalion were reservists who, prior to the Korean War, had no connection with the regiment in which they now served, but Lieutenant Colonel Carne, a quiet and reserved man, welded them into a thoroughly efficient fighting force.

In Korea, the battalion first chased after the North Korean army, fleeing from the might of the United Nations forces, then fought a rearguard action against the Chinese hordes which suddenly entered the war on behalf of the North Koreans.

James Power Carne

The Chinese were fanatical fighters who drove the forces of the United Nations back down the Korean peninsular until, in February, 1951, the United Nations' Force began to fight its way north once more, Colonel Carne personally leading his battalion on more than one occasion when it encountered particularly stiff resistance.

The advance reached the Imjim River where the battalion held a front of almost 6,000 metres against the Chinese who had turned and were once more on the offensive. The main task of the Gloucesters was to deny the enemy the use of the road which ran through their position, but on the 22nd April, the Chinese made contact and for the next three days attacked in ever increasing numbers.

It was soon apparent that the Chinese vastly outnumbered the Gloucesters (The figures were later given as some 27,000 Chinese attacking the thinly spread 750 soldiers of the Gloucestershire Regiment), but Colonel Carne's orders were to hold his position 'at all costs'.

Eventually, it was realised that the situation of the Gloucesters was hopeless and they were given an order to carry out a fighting withdrawal. This order was countermanded almost immediately and the Battalion was instructed to disperse and attempt to infiltrate back through the Chinese lines.

The order had come too late. The Gloucesters were surrounded in overwhelming numbers. A few were successful in making their way to safety, but 622 soldiers of the regiment were captured or killed – a number being murdered in cold blood by the Chinese.

During these traumatic hours Lieutenant Colonel Carne moved among his men, comforting and encouraging them until he too was taken prisoner.

A long period of captivity was to follow, but in the long march north and in the prison camps, Colonel Carne set such an example to his men, and to prisoners from the armies of other United Nations countries, that his captors moved him into solitary confinement, where he would spend the next nineteen months – nineteen months of almost unbearable loneliness and cruelty.

During his time in solitary confinement, and using makeshift tools, Colonel Carne succeeded in carving a Cornish cross in stone, which is now proudly exhibited in Gloucester Cathedral.

Not until October, 1953, did this very brave soldier return to England to be notified that he had been awarded a Victoria Cross. The United States also awarded him the highest honour open to a foreign officer, the Distinguished Service Cross and he was given the Freedom of Falmouth and of Gloucester.

Colonel Carne always protested that the Victoria Cross was an award to the whole of the 1st Battalion of the Gloucestershire Regiment, but there can be few officers who did more to make this prestigious award a personal honour.

When he retired from the army Colonel Carne spent his days in a quiet

Gloucestershire village, becoming a deputy lieutenant of his adopted county, living his life as the modest and reserved man who had so inspired the men who were proud to have served him in battle.

Colonel James Power Carne, VC, DSO, DL died in Cheltenham, Gloucestershire, on 19th April, 1986, little more than a week after his 80th birthday.

Stephen Halden Beattie 1908–1975

Stephen Halden Beattie, died on 24th April, 1975 and his memorial is in the peaceful churchyard of Ruan Minor, in Cornwall, only a few miles away from the place where, on 27 March, 1942, he had set sail on what many believed to be a suicidal mission.

The bitter war between Germany and Great Britain was in its third year and things were not going well for Britain and its allies. In the Far East, Malaya, Singapore, the Dutch East Indies, the Philippines and Burma had all fallen to the Japanese army, while, closer to home, Field Marshal Rommel appeared to have the beating of the Allied armies in North Africa.

At sea, German submarines – the dreaded 'U-boats' – were reaping a grim harvest among the ships bringing vital supplies to Britain's shores and together with surface ships led by the mighty battleship *Tirpitz* were decimating the convoys carrying essential war materials to Russia and posing a serious threat to the survival of Great Britain itself.

It was decided that something was needed to raise the morale of the beleaguered British people, at the same time striking a severe blow against the German navy.

In France, at St. Nazaire, on the River Loire, was the only dock outside Germany capable of taking the *Tirpitz* and it was decided it should be destroyed. The plan was for an old ship, the ex-American destroyer HMS *Campbeltown*, packed with three tons of explosive, to be taken across the channel to ram the outer gate of the entrance and blown up, thus denying access to the German battleship.

It was to be a night attack, the aged destroyer being escorted by a motor gunboat and a Motor Torpedo Boat. In addition, there would be some 16 motor launches carrying Commandos, whose task would be to land and destroy as many of the dock installations as was possible in the short time allowed for the operation.

The commanding officer of HMS *Campbeltown* was 34 year-old Lieutenant Commander Stephen Halden Beattie, an experienced destroyer officer, while Commander Robert Ryder was in overall command of the whole operation.

It was indeed a suicidal raid. According to Intelligence reports, opposing them in the St. Nazaire area were some 10,000 German troops. In addition, the five miles of estuary which needed to be negotiated by the raiders was one of the most heavily guarded areas in the whole of Nazi-occupied Europe.

The small flotilla set sail from Falmouth, in Cornwall, in the early hours of 27th March, 1942. Acting as escorts as far as the French coast were the destroyers *Atherstone* and *Tynedale* and both ships would remain off the coast to take on board any survivors from the raid.

It was a very small party for such a daring raid, no more than 353 naval officers and ratings, plus two hundred and sixty commandos – and their progress did not go unnoticed. They were spotted by a U-boat who reported the sighting, but the small British flotilla was able to get within two miles of their objective before they were actually challenged. It happened in the mouth of the River Loire, when *Campbeltown* was picked out by a German searchlight.

Before setting out on the raid, *Campbeltown* had been altered to give the ship the appearance of a German destroyer and, giving German identification signals in response to the challenge, *Campbeltown* gained precious minutes.

However, when the German searchlights picked out the small craft accompanying the British destroyer the deception was over and a withering fire was

Stephen Halden Beattie

poured into the flotilla from both banks of the Loire.

It was now 1.30am on the morning of 28th March and, calling for maximum speed, Beattie aimed his destroyer and its deadly cargo at the dock's caisson and rammed it with such force that a tenth of the destroyer's entire length penetrated inside the dock itself.

Meanwhile, all hell was breaking loose around the dock. The gunners on *Campbeltown* and the British launches were firing at the German gun positions, but the superior German fire power had the added advantage of searchlights to light up their targets. The Commandos, struggling to make their way ashore and get to grips with the enemy, were suffering heavy casualties.

By the time Commander Ryder ordered a withdrawal, no more than seven of the 16 launches were still afloat – and only three would return to Falmouth, although the destroyers *Atherstone* and *Tynedale* were able to rescue those on board the other four.

Only 40% of the raiding party returned to the United Kingdom, but the raid was a success in that it closed the dock to *Tirpitz* and showed the world how much could be achieved by a small, but determined, force.

Lieutenant Commander Beattie was taken prisoner by the Germans, together with 214 of the British raiders, but when *Campbeltown* blew up, some six hours later than had been planned, almost 400 German soldiers were killed and more would die the following day when torpedoes fired by the MTB exploded.

The raid itself resulted in a remarkable number of decorations being awarded in addition to the Victoria Cross awarded to Beattie. Two other VCs were won and there were also 2 DSOs; 17 DSCs; 11 MCs; 4 CGMs; 5 DCMs; 24 DSMs and 15 MMs, as well as 51 'mentioned in despatches'. Sadly, a great many of the awards were posthumous.

As well as taking part in a successful and daring raid, Lieutenant Commander Beattie and the men with him brightened what was a black year in wartime Britain.

Stephen Holden Beattie retired from the Royal Navy with the rank of Captain, spending his last years close to the port from which he set off on the raid that would go down in history for the courage of the men who took part and died in Cornwall on 24th April 1975.

Footnote: It would seem that bravery ran in the Beattie family. Reverend Ernest Halden Beattie, father of Stephen, was awarded the Military Cross in 1918 for conspicuous gallantry and devotion to duty as chaplain to the 140th Infantry Brigade and held the rank of lieutenant colonel when placed on the reserve list of officers.

Thomas Edward Rendle 1884–1946

Thomas Edward Rendle, born at Bedminster, Bristol, enlisted in the Duke of Cornwall's Light Infantry as a bandsman with the 1st Battalion, in 1912, when he was twenty-eight years of age.

As a peacetime bandsman, it was a good life for both Rendle and his wife. The band played at a great many regimental and civil functions which his wife would often attend, and she also became known as a sound and reliable nanny who was entrusted with the children of the senior officers of the regiment.

Then came the First World War, which would change everything. In wartime when the regiment was in action, bandsmen were required to put their instruments aside and assume the duties of stretcher-bearers – and so it was with Bandsman Rendle.

Among the first troops despatched to France was the 1st Battalion of the DCLI and they were involved in almost continuous fighting during those early critical weeks of the war. On the night of 17th November, 1914, the 1st Battalion took over from French troops a mile-long length of shallow front line trenches, often no more than mere ditches, which in places were less than 50 yards from the German lines.

The first thing the Battalion needed to do was to make the trenches deeper and wider and dig communication trenches to connect them with each other.

By 20th November the trenches were in a satisfactory state, but then, at 9am. the Germans began a heavy artillery bombardment. The British soldiers were at first delighted when the German guns scored three direct hits on their own trenches, but then their guns found their range and the next salvo landed on the parapet of a DCLI trench, burying some 15 men, while others were killed and many more severely wounded. The commanding officer of A Company was himself buried up to his neck and remained in this frightening situation while shells continued to rain down around him, demolishing some 40 yards of front line trenches.

Bandsman Rendle was prominent during this bombardment, working to free injured and wounded men and helping to get the many casualties away from the front line. In the words of a contemporary account:

Whilst heavy howitzers were dropping shells upon a trench occupied by the Duke of Cornwall Light Infantry at Wulverghem, Bandsman Thomas Edward Rendle was

*Thomas
Edward
Rendle*

attending to the rapidly increasing number of wounded. Suddenly a huge shell burst upon the parapet of a trench nearby, completely shattering the top and burying some men beneath the debris. Seeing that not a moment must be lost, Rendle rushed to the debris of the parapet and began scraping away the earth with his bare hands. His fingers were soon raw and bleeding with the haste and urgency with which he worked and he constantly exposed himself at a gap in the trench as he disposed of the earth. Though running great danger from the bullets of snipers, which constantly flew past his head, he laboured until every man was rescued...

The German barrage ceased for a while, but in the late afternoon it had resumed with increased ferocity and accuracy, when one of the A Company's officers, Second-Lieutenant Colebrooke, who was sitting at the bottom of a trench in an isolated section, was hit in the thigh by a sniper's bullet, which severed the main artery.

With one of the Regiment's officers, Rendle reached Colebrooke and succeeded in stemming the blood and bandaging his wounded leg. During this time, the parapet of the trench having been blown in, the men were in a frighteningly exposed position and were subjected to fire from both artillery and machine guns.

The shelling caused the parapet to collapse inwards on the trench for some considerable length and in order to get the wounded officer back to safety, Rendle began digging a shallow burrow. This could only be achieved by lying on his stomach and every time he lifted his body to throw away the soil the Germans opened fire on him. Nevertheless, when he had succeeded in excavating a shallow trench, Rendle took Colebrooke on his back and wriggled his way to safety, thus saving the life of Second-Lieutenant Colebrooke.

The award of the Victoria Cross was gazetted on 11th January, 1915, with the following citation:

For conspicuous bravery on 20th November 1914, near Wulverghem, when he attended to the wounded under heavy shell and rifle fire, and rescued men from the trenches in which they had been buried by the blowing in of the parapets by the fire of the enemy's heavy howitzers.

In 1920, now a bandmaster sergeant, Thomas Rendle was invalided out of the army and emigrated to South Africa, where he would later become bandmaster to the Duke of Edinburgh's Own Rifles. He died at Groote Schuur Hospital, Cape Town on 1st June, 1946, aged 63 years and was buried in Maitland Cemetery, Cape Town.

He has the honour of being the recipient of the only Victoria Cross awarded to a serving member of the Duke of Cornwall's Light Infantry during the First World War and he also ended the war with a 'mention in despatches' and the Russian Order of St George, 4th Class.

Guy Penrose Gibson 1918–1944

Strangely, for a region that has been renowned throughout its history for breeding men of a buccaneering spirit, the West Country has a dearth of Royal Air Force personnel who have been awarded a Victoria Cross.

However, the man with whom it can claim a close association is one of the legendary heroes of World War II, his exploits the subject of a great many books and articles, and immortalised in a highly successful film, *The Dam Busters*.

Guy Gibson was born in India on 12th August, 1918, the youngest of three children to Alexander and Leonora Gibson. At the time of his birth, his father was a 42 year-old senior official of the Indian Forestry Service, and his mother a 23 year-old from Porthleven, in Cornwall.

In a strange way it was a very cosmopolitan family. Guy's father, Alexander, came from a family which had served in India for generations although he had, in fact, been born in Russia. Leonora – who preferred to be called Nora – completed her education in a Belgian convent and their three children were all born in India, where they were cosseted by a small army of servants.

In 1922, Nora brought her children back to Porthleven on holiday, to introduce them to their many Cornish relatives. Two years later mother and children were back again, this time because the Gibson children were to be placed in boarding schools – and Nora Gibson would remain in the country too.

While attending various boarding schools, Guy and his brother and sister would spend their school holidays at Porthleven with their grandparents and this would be the nearest thing to a permanent home Guy would know for the remainder of his brief life.

It was while at public school in Oxford that Guy decided he wanted to fly and he applied for a Short Service Commission in the Royal Air Force – but they turned him down!

The rejection was probably because he was rather small in stature. However, with a determination that was to surface again in later years, Guy Gibson refused to accept defeat and when he applied again the RAF relented. In November 1936, he entered the Service and on 31st January, 1937, became a student pilot at Netheravon , in Wiltshire.

In May he was awarded his 'wings' and later in the year went on a course for prospective bomber pilots. As a result, in November, 1937 he was posted to a bomber squadron, flying biplanes.

In 1938 and into early 1939, the squadron was re-equipped with a new single wing, twin-engined bomber, the Handley Page Hampden – and 1939 would prove a momentous year for the young Guy Gibson.

In September, Great Britain declared war on Germany. It was to be a war in which Guy Gibson would carve himself an indelible place in history. In December he met Evelyn Moore, a professional dancer, seven years his senior and in the same month his mother died in tragic circumstances in a London hospital.

Guy Gibson's squadron became increasingly involved in the war during 1940 and in July he was awarded his first Distinguished Flying Cross. Later in the year he moved from bombers to night fighting Beaufighters and, in November, he and Evelyn Moore were married.

Although there can be no doubt that Guy was besotted with his new wife, he was also a totally dedicated pilot – and the two were not always compatible. In September, 1941, he was awarded a Bar to his DFC, the citation praising his 'Utmost courage and devotion to duty, having destroyed three enemy aircraft and damaged a fourth.'

He had also advanced from flying officer to acting squadron leader and, in the Spring of 1942, the squadron with which he was now flying began to take delivery of a new 4-engined bomber with which the name of Guy Gibson would forever be inextricably linked. The new aircraft from the Avro factory was named, the 'Lancaster'.

In the Lancaster, Guy Gibson clocked up an impressive number of flying hours and as his skill with piloting this giant aircraft improved, so did recognition of those skills. In November, 1942, he was awarded the Distinguished Service Order and in March 1943 a bar to the DSO.

In the same month, now a Wing Commander, Guy Gibson was asked to form a new Lancaster squadron at Scampton, in Lincolnshire. It would subsequently be numbered '617 Squadron' and would carve a niche in history – as the 'Dambusters'.

The majority of the crews for this elite squadron were chosen by Gibson himself, but if they did not measure up to his demanding requirements, they were quickly moved on.

Guy Gibson was not fully aware of the purpose of this new squadron until he was introduced to a Vickers' engineer by the name of Barnes Wallis, who had developed a new weapon – a form of depth charge – which it was felt could be dropped from a low height and, using incredible precision, skip across the water until it sank against the wall of one of the might Ruhr dams and exploded, demolishing the dam wall and flooding the valley below and with it the many vitally important factories of the Ruhr.

Guy Penrose Gibson

The task faced by the squadron would be formidable and one involving almost impossible precision. For the operation to succeed, the four-engined Lancasters would be required to dive to 150 feet in an enclosed and heavily defended valley at night and drop their specially designed 'bouncing bombs' at a precise speed of 240 mph.

The operation was not made easier by the fact that Guy Gibson would not know exact details of the targets until the very last minute – and in the meantime had no more than two months in which to train his crews in what would be an incredible display of precision flying.

There were many problems to be overcome. The design of the bouncing bombs, the difficulty in maintaining the precise height essential for the success of these unorthodox weapons and the welding of the squadron into a super-efficient unit.

The success of the latter was achieved as much by the sheer personality of Guy Gibson as by any other means and on 16th May, 1943, the squadron was told the attack would take place that night.

Just before 9.30pm the first of 19 Lancasters took off from the airfield at Scampton, their revolutionary bouncing bombs slung beneath them. Eight would never return.

At least two of the Lancasters never even reached the dam, the first returning to Scampton only twenty minutes after the last of 617 Squadron took off on their historic mission.

Even finding the dams at night was an incredible piece of navigation. Attacking them in the face of fierce anti-aircraft fire was daunting, but Gibson did this not once, but four times. Dropping his own bouncing bomb, he then flew to one side and slightly ahead of the next three aircraft to attack the Mohne dam, drawing the fire from the attacking Lancester, until the dam was breached.

He then flew on with the next wave of Lancasters which successfully destroyed a second dam, the Eder, situated among a myriad of hills and lakes.

It was 4.15am when Gibson and his Lancaster touched down at Scampton, to be jubilantly greeted by some of the most senior officers in the Royal Air Force. The success of the raid would be celebrated in the newspapers of Great Britain and its allies across the world. Guy Gibson had become a hero.

But the hero spent much of the next day writing letters of condolence to the next-of-kin of the fifty-six airmen who did not return.

The award of a Victoria Cross to Guy Gibson was gazetted on 28th May, 1943 and thirty-three members of 617 Squadron were also honoured for their part in a skilful and daring raid which had captured the imagination not only of a nation, but of the world.

Guy Gibson would now go on to be feted in all of the countries which stood with Great Britain in the war against Germany and in America he would have the rare honour of being awarded the United States Legion of Merit.

As a pilot, Guy Gibson had seen more than one man's share of action and should have lived out the remainder of the war resting on his laurels and being feted wherever he went – but this was not the way of the man.

That year Guy spent a holiday in Cornwall with Eve, who found the moods of her hero husband difficult to predict – not surprising in view of all that had happened to him.

However, Guy's first love was still, as it had always been – flying – and on 19th September, 1944, although not officially an operational pilot, he took off in a twin-engined Mosquito fighter-bomber on an operational flight over Germany, dropping flares to illuminate the target for an attack by Lancaster bombers.

He did not return.

Soon after 11.30 pm that night his Mosquito crashed and exploded on the outskirts of the Dutch town of Steenbergen, the violence of the explosion and the subsequent fire being so fierce that little remained of either the aircraft or the two man crew.

Wing Commander Guy Penrose Gibson, VC, DSO & Bar, DFC & Bar, Legion of Merit, was only 26 years of age when he died on the night of 19th September, 1944, but the legend he left behind him will never die for as long as the Victoria Cross is recognised as the ultimate badge of courage.

Philip Kenneth Edward Curtis 1926–1951

The most recent soldier of the Duke of Cornwall Light Infantry to be awarded the Victoria Cross, Philip Curtis had a brief, glorious, yet tragic life.

Born on 7th July, 1926 in Devonport, a port used by the Royal Navy since 1691, Curtis had just become a teenager at the outbreak of World War II.

Eager to play a part in the conflict, he became a messenger for the ARP (Air Raid Precaution) Wardens during the horrendous bombing campaign launched against Plymouth by the German Luftwaffe during the early years of World War II.

Because of Devonport's close ties with the Royal Navy, Curtis might have been expected to join that service when he became of age. Instead, and perhaps because of his experiences during the blitz on Plymouth, he tried to join the Royal Air Force in 1942, when he was only 16 years old.

Rejected because of his age, he was forced to wait until he was 18 when he joined neither the Royal Navy, nor the Royal Air Force – but the army. However, much to his disappointment he was never posted to an operational theatre of war.

Nevertheless, in May 1946 he gained a commission in the Duke of Cornwall Light Infantry and saw service with the Royal Army Service Corps before he was demobilised in 1948 and placed on the Officers' Reserve List.

By this time, Curtis had married Joan Haynes, also from Devonport and they had a daughter, Phillipa Susan. Life seemed to be settling down for Philip Curtis and his family, then suddenly, in 1950, Joan Curtis died. Before he had time to adjust to his loss, the army of North Korea invaded their neighbours to the south and a war began which would soon involve the United Nations, opposing not only North Korea but also the vast armies of China.

Britain mobilised its reservists, and Philip Curtis was numbered among them.

It is certain that with responsibility for a young daughter Philip Curtis could have claimed exemption, but that was not in his character. Besides, the loss of his wife had already turned his life upside down. When his mother-in-law offered to take care of his young daughter, he was able to go off to war with a clear conscience and so, on 17th October, 1950, Lieutenant Philip Curtis set sail for Korea, seconded to the 1st Battalion of the Gloucestershire Regiment – the 'Glorious Gloucesters'.

Delayed in Japan by bureaucracy, Curtis finally succeeded in joining A Company of the 1st Battalion the Gloucesters, on 3rd March, 1951 and it was not long before he saw action with them.

The army in Korea had seen the battle lines ebb and flow time and time again along the whole Korean peninsular. In March it was the turn of the United Nation forces to advance and this they did, reaching the Imjim River, in the vicinity of the 38th parallel, where they temporarily came to a halt and dug in while the politicians, far from the war itself, sought a political settlement of the war.

A settlement was not achieved and in late April, A Company of the Gloucesters was occupying a position known as Castle Hill, the highest point of which, known as 'Castle Site', was where an ancient castle had once dominated the area. Now grassy mounds hid the remnants of ancient walls.

Nearby was a crossing of the Imjim River which would later become known as Gloucester Crossing and the Gloucesters, no more than a few hundred strong, were to the south of the river.

Opposing them to the north, were many thousands of Chinese infantrymen, poised to launch an attack across the Imjim River.

The hill was a vital, if exposed stronghold, with too great an area defended by too few men and the key to the whole position was Castle Site. Should this be lost, the positions of the Gloucesters would be untenable.

For a few days all seemed quiet in the vicinity of Castle Hill and the soldiers began to believe that rumours of a Chinese attack were unfounded, especially as air reconnaissance had revealed no Chinese army. However, aware of the awesome power of United Nation air strikes, the Chinese had become masters at moving at night and cleverly hiding themselves during the day.

On the night of 21st/22nd April, there was a skirmish at the river crossing, in which three men of the Gloucesters drove back a Chinese patrol of 14 men, killing or wounding half of them.

On the 22nd, a Gloucester patrol sent over the river saw a small group of enemy soldiers, but the Chinese did not seem to be in the area in any significant numbers. Then, that same afternoon, a number of small parties of Chinese were spotted among the hills across the river but they were swiftly scattered by mortar fire.

That evening, Lieutenant Colonel Carne, Commanding Officer of the 1st Battalion ordered that a strong patrol be positioned at the crossing when darkness fell.

There was an unusual air of expectancy among the Gloucesters which began to fade as time went by without anything happening. Then, at 10.30pm, the soldiers on Castle Hill saw a series of flashes from Gloucester Crossing,

Philip Kenneth Edward Curtis

accompanied by the sound of heavy automatic weapons. The Gloucester patrol was under attack.

Soon the noise of battle was continuous and now artillery attached to the Gloucesters, together with their own mortars, began pounding the north bank of the river. The battle raged on with increasing ferocity until, at midnight, the patrol at the crossing was forced to pull back.

Meanwhile, on Castle Hill, Lieutenant Curtis was only a listener to the ferocious sounds of battle. He and his platoon of some 30 men were 'in reserve', waiting to be sent where they were most needed, when it became possible to ascertain what would be required of them.

For some six hours the battle raged and as dawn approached it became apparent that one of the Gloucester platoons was in serious trouble. Their ammunition low, most of the men had been killed or wounded and part of their position overrun by the Chinese.

What was even more serious, the Chinese had managed to position machine guns near the crest of Castle Site – and if Castle Site fell the Gloucesters would have lost the battle.

Colonel Carne was contacted by radio explaining the Company's perilous position and requesting that reinforcements be sent to them.

Colonel Carne's reply was chillingly clear. A Company would remain on the hill at all costs until further notice and at about 5am, Curtis and his reserve platoon were told to mount a counter-attack on Castle Site. The orders were explicit. With his platoon he would retake Castle Site – and hold it.

At first light, Curtis's men left their trenches and fixed bayonets. Then, leading his men, Curtis advanced up the hill to one of the ridges. All seemed disturbingly quiet. Suddenly a large number of Chinese soldiers stood up, some still clutching the bushes they had been holding as a very effective camouflage.

The Gloucesters dropped to the ground and using small arms and grenades engaged the Chinese in a furious battle.

The small platoon was hopelessly outnumbered and before long Curtis became concerned that the Chinese would encircle them. Another great concern was that a bunker on Castle Hill, built by the Americans during the ebb and flow battles earlier in the war was now occupied by a Chinese machine gun, firing at virtually point-blank range.

Dashing across open ground to his platoon sergeant, Curtis told him to take the reserve section of the platoon – about ten men – and engage any Chinese coming up the hill from the direction of a village some distance away.

Then, gathering a few men about him, Curtis worked his way under intense fire to a point only some 20 metres from the bunker. The machine gun was clearly visible through the apertures in the bunker and so too were the gunners.

Curtis began hurling grenades at the bunker, in a bid to lob one through an aperture. In this he was unsuccessful and the machine gunners quickly turned their attention upon Curtis's men, forcing them to seek cover.

Only Curtis remained, defying the machine gun fire as he lobbed grenade after grenade, all the while attempting to move closer. It was almost inevitable that by exposing himself in such a way he would be hit. Sure enough, a bullet struck him in the head, knocking him over and he lay exposed, only a few metres from the bunker.

Two of his men wriggled forward and succeeded in dragging him back to cover and a soldier was despatched to fetch a medical orderly, while his men bandaged his head with a field dressing.

Although his face and head were covered in blood, Curtis was conscious and insisted that the attack should be continued. So insistent was he that the soldiers had to hold him down, one of them even sitting on him to try to prevent him from personally going on the offensive once more.

Suddenly, Curtis succeeded in throwing them off and, hurling grenades ahead of him, staggered towards the still firing machine gun until, when only a few metres from the bunker he was mortally wounded in the stomach by a burst of machine gun fire.

However, as one of his platoon later stated, even as he fell he threw his last grenade – and suddenly the machine gun fell silent. As a result, the remainder of Lieutenant Curtis's platoon were able to secure Castle Site.

Curtis was still alive when he was carried back to the medical orderly, but by the time he arrived he was past all human help and died in the arms of the soldiers who had carried him down the slope.

By now there was only one officer left alive on Castle Hill and at 8.15am, Lieutenant Colonel Carne gave permission for the fifty-four survivors of A Company to pull back some 3,000 metres to a position known as Hill 235. It fell to Sergeant-Major Gallagher to organise the withdrawal, a feat that would earn him a Distinguished Conduct Medal.

Philip Curtis's body was not recovered for six weeks and his posthumous Victoria Cross not gazetted until December, 1953, when witnesses to his bravery, including Lieutenant Colonel Carne, himself awarded a Victoria Cross, were released from Chinese prisoner-of-war camps, where they had been held for more than two years.

It was stated that Curtis's actions enabled the Chinese attack on Castle Site to be driven off for sufficient time to permit the withdrawal of the company, thus averting many more casualties.

Lieutenant Philip Curtis's Victoria Cross was presented to his daughter by Queen Elizabeth II at Buckingham Palace on 6 July, 1954 and is now exhibited in the DCLI Museum, at Bodmin, in proud recognition of the deeds of a very brave man.

Gordon Charles Steele 1894–1981

At eleven o'clock in the morning of the eleventh day of the eleventh month of 1918, an Armistice came into force in Europe, silencing the guns which had caused such slaughter during four years of war, and ending the danger and misery of the soldiers who occupied opposing trenches.

But the war was not over for everyone, and not all the armed forces of Germany were brought to heel. A bloody revolution was taking place in Russia that threatened the stability of the nations that had so recently been at war with one another.

There were areas around Russia's borders that were in a state of utter confusion and none more so than in the countries bordering the Baltic Sea. The many states here were divided – or linked – by ethnic origins, religion, national fervour and alliances, many of which changed on an almost daily basis. In addition, the Bolshevik threat from Russia itself threatened to engulf many of the smaller countries.

It was because of this threat that the German army and a small navy were allowed, within limits, to continue their presence. So, in the Baltic Sea there was a very powerful Russian naval presence, a much smaller German naval force – and a British Fleet.

It was into this hopelessly confused situation that Rear Admiral Walter Cowan arrived in 1919, despatched to the area by a government which had no clear policy for the area and seemed undecided about who was friend and who was foe.

It was an impossible situation for any commander who, in addition to his other responsibilities had been told to give all possible assistance to two British Coastal Motor Boats being operated in secret in the area by a British naval officer, on behalf of the British Secret Service.

One of the few policies clear to Cowan was that the British government was supporting anti-Bolshevik Russians against the Communist revolutionaries. So, when Bolshevik Russian ships began shelling a 'White' Russian stronghold, Cowan sanctioned a covert operation against them by the two small Coastal Motor Boats carrying out secret missions under the command of Lieutenant Agar RN.

In the event only one of the motor boats succeeded in entering the heavily fortified island harbour at Kronstadt, where the Communist Russian fleet was

Gordon Charles Steele

based, but it torpedoed and sank a 6,700 ton cruiser, under the very noses of the Bolshevik authorities.

It was an audacious raid that won a Victoria Cross for Lieutenant Agar. It also gave Admiral Cowan an idea of how he might deal with two Russian battleships based at Kronstadt, which were able to pound White Russian positions at will and also posed a serious threat to his fleet should they choose to emerge and attack him.

Kronstadt was protected by a number of heavily armed forts forming a chain between the island where the Russian harbour was situated, and the mainland. There were also extensive minefields and underwater breakwaters. Without charts of the minefields and the breakwaters, only vessels of very shallow draught could attempt to enter the harbour – as Agar had done.

In view of this, Cowan arranged for a number of Coastal Motor Boats to be sent out from England, his intention being to use them to mount a daring raid on the capital ships hiding in the Kronstadt naval base.

Eight Coastal Motor Boats, of a type slightly larger than those used by Agar, were towed out from their base near Clacton, in Essex. Unfortunately, bad weather sank one boat, and the tow ropes of the others were constantly breaking, but seven CMB s reached Cowan's base in the Finnish port of Biorko at the end of July. Their commanding officer was Commander Claude Congreve Dobson. In the days following his arrival, Dobson carried out a number of reconnaissance flights over Kronstadt to check out the harbour for himself and ascertain where the two Bolshevik battleships were berthed.

It was decided that the depot ship *Pamyat Azova* should be targeted at the same time, in order to curtail the activities of Bolshevik submarines, which had already successfully attacked Cowan's fleet. There were also at least three cruisers inside the harbour and, immediately outside the entrance, a Bolshevik destroyer was stationed to act as a guard ship.

An attack by the tiny three-man Coastal Motor Boats against such formidable opposition appeared to be foolhardy, but by the middle of August, the plans had been drawn up and everything was ready for the audacious raid – everything except the weather. However, the weather proved to be perfect on Sunday, 17th August 1919 and the raid was arranged at short notice for that night.

On board each CMB, the crew was comprised of a commanding officer who would be at the wheel, a second officer responsible for firing the torpedoes, and a mechanic to tend the vessels twin engines. The boats also carried a local smuggler to act as a pilot should the need arise – a precaution which proved a wise one.

Lieutenant Agar VC, had been called in to guide the boats to Kronstadt between the forts but during the night run three of the boats lost touch with him, including the boat of Commander Dobson, whose smuggler passenger took him on a different route before he was able to rejoin his other boats, just off the Bolshevik held island.

Along the way some of the forts opened fire on the boats, but they appeared to be unaware of the significance of so many motor vessels and Kronstadt was not warned of their approach.

The CMBs formed up into two groups, the first led by Lieutenant Bremner, who carried apparatus to deal with a boom, should there be one across the harbour entrance. There was not and as aircraft of the Royal Air Force arrived to create a diversion, Bremner went straight in and attacked the submarine depot ship. His torpedoes struck home and the depot ship sank almost immediately.

Commander Dobson was next and in order to fire his torpedoes needed to manoeuvre his boat by stopping one engine in order to make a very tight turn, but his torpedoes also found their target, the battle-cruiser *Petrapavlovsk*, which began to settle in the waters of the harbour. Unfortunately, the sound of the explosions brought out the garrison, who had been sheltering from the bombs dropped by the RAF.

As the third boat, captained by Lieutenant Dayrell-Reed entered the harbour it was fired upon from all sides but continued to head towards the berths of the large warships.

Suddenly, the second officer on board, Lieutenant Gordon Steele, realised that the CMB was heading straight for a hospital ship. He called to warn Dayrell-Reed, but saw him slumped over the wheel. He had been shot in the head.

Jumping to the wheel, Steele lowered the commanding officer into the cockpit, at the same time spinning the wheel to put the boat back on its proper course. They were now very close to the battleship, *Andrei Pervosvanni* and Steele manoeuvred the boat into position before firing his two torpedoes at very close range.

Steele's attack too was successful and he was so close to his target that water and powder from the explosion of the torpedoes was deposited upon the small British vessel before it headed at full speed for the harbour entrance under heavy fire and caught in the light of searchlights, which were promptly attacked by the RAF aircraft.

By now the defences in Kronstadt and on the nearby forts were thoroughly aroused and the CMB detailed to deal with the Bolshevik guardship was itself sunk by a shell from the destroyer.

Next, two of the CMBs collided in the entrance to the harbour, one almost being cut in two. By putting on full speed, the commanding officer of the surviving CMB was able to leave the harbour, carrying the more seriously damaged vessel with it until the crew were rescued. Unfortunately, the surviving boat was then sunk by the Russian guardship

Another of the CMBs broke down but was towed clear of Kronstadt and brought to safety.

Lieutenant Dayrell-Reed lived long enough to be congratulated by Admiral Cowan on the success of the mission, but died soon afterwards.

Three of the seven Coastal Motor Boats had been lost and a number of officers either killed or wounded. In addition, three officers and six ratings had been captured, but as a result of the operation a battleship, a battle-cruiser and a submarine depot ship had been sunk. The raid had been an outstanding success and the Bolshevik navy no longer posed a serious threat to Admiral Cowan's fleet.

Two Victoria Crosses were awarded as a result of this audacious raid. One went to Commander Dobson for his leadership, skill and bravery in commanding the operation. The second went to Lieutenant Gordon Charles Steele for his courage and presence of mind when the commanding officer of his boat was fatally injured, and for carrying on to sink the Russian battleship *Andrei Pervosvanni.*

Gordon Steele was born at Exeter, in Devon, on 1st November, 1894, the son of a Royal Navy captain, and was a cadet on HMS *Worcester*, a training ship moored on the River Thames. He became a Merchant Navy officer and also, in 1909, a Midshipman in the Royal Naval Reserve.

When the Great War broke out, he joined the Royal Navy and had an adventurous service life. After a brief spell in a battleship, he served first on submarines, then on 'Q' Ships, the decoy vessels which were deployed to counter the German U-boat menace. Mentioned in despatches, he was promoted lieutenant and served in the battleship *Royal Oak*, at the Battle of Jutland and later had command of two small vessels before taking part in the Kronstadt raid.

Retiring from the Royal Navy on half-pay in 1929, he became Captain Superintendent of his old Training Ship, the *Worcester*, until his retirement in 1957, when he held the rank of commander, RN.

Commander Gordon Charles Steele, VC, died at Winkleigh, Devon on 4th January, 1981 after a long, gallant and eventful life.

George Hinkley 1819–1904

To the ordinary soldier and sailor, the causes for which they fought in the wars of past centuries must at times have seemed confusing, but few can have been more difficult to comprehend than the wars in China during the middle years of the 19th century.

Until the end of 1860 the armies and navies of Britain and France had fought against the forces of Imperial China in an on-again, off-again war. Yet, shortly afterwards the same British soldiers and sailors were fighting alongside the Imperial Chinese army against a rebel Chinese army, that of the Taiping, whose leader laid claims to being the younger brother of Jesus Christ, and who had once been regarded as a potential ally of the Europeans.

The Taiping rebellion was one of the bloodiest in history, it being estimated that no fewer than 20,000,000 people died as a result of this bitter conflict. At first, the only non-Chinese forces fighting the Taiping were mercenaries, led by an American, Frederick Ward. So successful was Ward that the Imperial Chinese authorities gave his troops the name of 'The Ever-Victorious Army'.

When Ward died, relations between the Imperial Chinese and the Europeans had improved so much that they eventually requested a British officer be sent to take his place. The man chosen was a Royal Engineer, Captain Charles Gordon – 'Chinese Gordon' – later to achieve fame in, death, as 'General Gordon, of Khartoum'.

But before Gordon took command, the Ever-Victorious Army was reinforced in early October, 1862, by a French naval force, together with a Naval Brigade formed of sailors from the crews of the British ships *Sphinx*, *Encounter*, *Flamer* and *Hardy*.

Their objective was the fortified town of Fung Wha, almost fifty kilometres distant, and close to the great port of Shanghai. It was to be a testing journey, the roads being either bad, or non-existent – and it rained incessantly. Nevertheless, the whole force, British, French and Chinese, reached their destination and took up positions before the main gate of the walled town and the attack got under way.

First to go into action were the Chinese of the late Frederick Ward's Ever-Victorious Army, but on this occasion they failed to live up to their name. They were driven off by the Taiping defenders after suffering heavy losses.

George Hinkley

Next it was the turn of the naval brigade, among whom was Able Seaman Hinckley, of HMS *Sphinx*. With a number of soldiers of the Ever-Victorious Army, they attacked the main gate, only to discover that the defenders had successfully barricaded it from the inside and the attackers were subjected to a hail of musket balls fired by the defenders, and a barrage of heavy missiles thrown from the wall above.

Eventually, the attackers were forced to draw back, leaving very many dead and wounded men lying in front of the main gate.

Among the wounded was the assistant master of the *Sphinx*. Recognising him and ignoring the fact that the ground between the retreating sailors and the gate was under heavy fire from the walls of the town, Hinckley ran to the gate. Raising the wounded man, he hoisted him to his shoulder and ran with him to the comparative safety of a joss house – a Chinese temple – some distance away.

Then, aware that one of the European officers of The Ever-Victorious Army was also lying wounded in front of the gate, Hinckley once more braved death to run back and carry the second man to safety in a similar fashion.

With so many weapons being fired at him from the walls of Fung Wha, it was miraculous that Hinckley was not killed, but he survived to receive a Victoria

Cross for his selfless bravery from the Commander-in-Chief, Plymouth, at a ceremony in Devonport in July, 1863

Born in Liverpool on 22nd June, 1819, Hinckley had a somewhat chequered career in the navy, having served a twenty-eight day sentence of imprisonment only months before his actions gained him a VC.

Nevertheless, he was eventually promoted to the rank of quartermaster and in July, 1865, married a farmer's daughter at Stoke Damerel church in Devon and would retire from the Royal Navy on a pension.

George Hinckley lived out the remainder of his life in Devonport, dying in Plymouth in December, 1904 at the age of eighty-five.

Ernest Herbert Pitcher 1888–1946

Although, far more often than not, the deed for which a Victoria Cross is awarded is very much an individual act of bravery, there are occasions when a body of soldiers, sailors, or airmen, together perform acts of bravery that, collectively, are worthy of the supreme award for valour.

Section 13 of the original warrant for the Victoria Cross made provision for this by authorising that when such incidents occur, the recipient of the award could be selected by his peers. Officers would choose an officer, and those in the ranks would choose one of their own.

Ernest Pitcher was awarded his Victoria Cross in this way – and it was the second occasion on which he had been involved in such a ballot.

Pitcher was born at Mullion, in Cornwall on the last day of December, 1888, the son of a coastguard who later moved to Swanage in Dorset, where Pitcher went to school before joining the Royal Navy as a boy at Portsmouth in July, 1903.

A member of the crew of a dreadnought when World War I broke out, the following year saw him serving on a Q-ship. Manned by volunteers, the Q-ships were in effect decoy ships. Converted small steamers and sailing ships, they were to all intents and purposes unarmed small vessels unable to defend themselves. In fact they had guns concealed in deck houses and also carried torpedoes and depth charges.

Q-ships were introduced in a bid to combat the increasing menace of German submarines – U-boats – which were sinking an alarming amount of British shipping in the days before the adoption of a convoy system.

The introduction of Q-ships was kept a closely guarded secret but because they were deliberately trying to tempt a U-boat to attack them, they performed a highly dangerous task. It is little wonder that those officers and crew who survived the war could boast a great many medals between them.

Probably the most successful and best known of the Q-ship captains was Gordon Campbell, who had led a fairly uneventful life until as a lieutenant commander he took command of an ex-collier, renamed *Farnborough*, which had been fitted out as a Q-ship.

Early on a March morning in 1916, *Farnborough* was attacked by an unsuspecting U-boat which, after missing its target with a torpedo, surfaced to finish off the collier with gunfire as the crew apparently deserted their ship in a

Ernest Herbert Pitcher

show of panic. Instead, it was the U-boat which was swiftly despatched and sent to the bottom of the Atlantic with no survivors.

For this kill Campbell was awarded the first of his three DSOs and promoted to the rank of commander.

It was almost a year later, in February, 1917, off the West coast of Ireland when *Farnborough*, now designated Q5, was attacked by another U-boat. This time the ex-collier was struck by the torpedo and the hurried abandonment of Q5 was not entirely without cause. However, the gun crews remained on board, as did the engine room staff, even when sea water had flooded the engine-room almost to the level of the upper deck.

Convinced he had delivered a mortal blow to Q5, the U-boat commander surfaced and made for the boats that had quitted the ex-collier. It was a fatal error. At point blank range the concealed gunners on the Q-ship opened fire and sent the U-boat to the bottom of the ocean, only two of her crew being saved.

It seemed that Q5 was also doomed, but two Royal Navy vessels reached the scene quickly and, taking the Q-ship in tow, managed to eventually beach her. Campbell received the VC for this exploit, his first lieutenant was awarded the DSO and among the other awards was a 'mention in despatches' for Petty Officer Pitcher.

The crews of the Q-ships were allowed to leave their vessels and return to more normal duties at any time but Campbell's crew elected to stay with him when he took up his next command. Their latest vessel was another collier which had been renamed *Pergust* and fitted out with many of the items Campbell's experience had taught him would improve the efficiency of a Q-ship.

In June 1917, three months after commissioning, *Pergust* was torpedoed when in the Atlantic. The vessel was apparently abandoned, the crew having taken to the boats, accompanied by a stuffed parrot in a cage, and the U-boat cruised around the stricken vessel until, believing it really was no more than a collier, surfaced.

Once again, at point blank range, *Pergust's* guns opened fire and, after a furious barrage, the submarine exploded and sank.

This was the first occasion on which Pitcher's name went into a ballot for the VC, as two were awarded to the whole ship. The result of the ballots was that Lieutenant Stuart, DSO, received one and Seaman Williams, DSM, the other. Commander Campbell received his second DSO and promotion to Captain – and Petty Officer Pitcher was awarded the Distinguished Service Medal.

Pergust was successfully towed to Plymouth, but was beyond repair and the crew, with the exception of Lieutenant Stuart, who was given command of his own Q-ship, transferred to another converted collier, the *Dunraven*.

The *Dunraven* sailed from Cardiff on 4th August, 1917 and Campbell took his small ship to the Bay of Biscay, where U-boats had been particularly active. Sure enough, *Dunraven* attracted the attention of a U-boat only four days later.

This U-boat, more cautious than most, opened fire upon *Dunraven* at long-range and for three hours a cat-and-mouse battle ensued during which the Q-ship was struck by shells from the U-boat's gun and eventually 'abandoned', leaving the gun crews on board.

Unfortunately, although the German submarine was closing on the British vessel, it was still firing and scored a number of hits, including one which started a fire – and Pitcher and his gun crew were positioned immediately above an ammunition compartment!

Soon, the deck beneath them became so hot that Pitcher and the others were forced to lift boxes of cordite off the deck and hold them on their knees to prevent them from exploding.

Eventually, just as the U-boat was coming within close range to present an easy target, the inevitable happened. There was a huge explosion on board *Dunraven* and the 4-inch gun and its crew were blown into the air as exploding ammunition rained around them.

Pitcher was badly injured and the U-boat crash dived. Campbell returned to *Dunraven* to help the injured men when the German submarine scored a hit with a torpedo attack before surfacing once more.

There was a brief exchange between the two vessels before the U-boat dived once more as help arrived for *Dunraven* in the form of British and American destroyers.

Dunraven was taken in tow by the destroyer *Christopher*, but sank during the night.

Pitcher's name was once more put into the hat for a ballot for a VC – and this time he was successful. He would also receive the French Medaille Militaire and the Croix de Guerre to add to his DSM and MID.

Pitcher ended his service as a chief petty officer and retired from the navy after almost twenty-five years service in December, 1927.

At the outbreak of World War II he rejoined the Royal Navy and remained in the service until this very brave Cornishman died of tuberculosis in a Royal Naval hospital at Sherborne on 10th February, 1946.

Teignmouth Melvill 1842-1879

Until the conclusion of the Anglo-Boer War (1899-1902) the Victoria Cross was not awarded posthumously. However, a number of such awards were made for this conflict and it prompted an official review of previous recommendations made in respect of those who had performed deeds which would have been rewarded with the VC, had they survived.

Among their number was Lieutenant Teignmouth Melvill, of the 1st Battalion of the 24th Regiment (later to become the South Wales Borderers). In a memorandum in the London Gazette of 2nd May 1879, it was reported that for his attempt to save the Queen's Colour of his Regiment 'He would have been recommended to Her Majesty for the Victoria Cross, had he survived'.

But Teignmouth Melvill did not survive. He was killed by the warriors of Zulu king Cetshwayo when they overwhelmed a British column moving against them, slaughtering more than 1,300 soldiers and sending a shockwave through a horrified British Empire.

Born in London on 8th September 1842, Melvill's father was an East India Company official and his mother the daughter of a senior army officer whose home was in Helston, Cornwall. The family moved to Ethy House, situated South of Lostwithiel, in Cornwall, and, after attending school at Cheltenham and Harrow, the young Melvill went on to gain a Bachelor of Arts degree at Cambridge in 1865.

In that same year he purchased a commission as an ensign in the 24th Regiment and served with them in Ireland, being promoted to lieutenant late in 1868. In 1875 he travelled with the 1st Battalion to South Africa and for the next few years was involved in the various battles that took place between the British army and the various tribes of that part of the world.

However, not all Melvill's time in South Africa was taken up with war. In Port Elizabeth, Cape Colony he met Sarah Elizabeth Reed, twelve years his junior, and they were married in February 1876, when she was twenty years of age.

They were to enjoy less than three years of married life and it is doubtful whether Melvill ever knew his second son, Charles William, who was born at Ethy House during September 1878. He would also have seen little of his first son, born in February 1877.

Whilst in Africa Melvill had passed the entrance examination for the Staff College and travelled back to England early in 1878 to attend a course. With him

Teignmouth Melvill

was his pregnant wife, Sarah, and their oldest child, also named Teignmouth. However, when news was received of the outbreak of fresh hostilities in Africa he left his wife and child in England and returned to Africa in time to join the ill-fated central column of Lord Chelmford's army, marching against the Zulu armies of King Cetshwayo.

On 5th September that year, Sarah gave birth to her second son and he was baptised 'Charles William Melvill' in the Cornish church of St. Winnow, on the banks of the River Fowey, close to Ethy House.

It is apparent from contemporary accounts that Lord Chelmsford, the Commander-in-Chief of the British army in South Africa, grossly underestimated the fighting capabilities of the highly disciplined Zulu impis.

When Chelmsford entered Zululand with his army formed into three columns, he was unaware that a 20,000 strong Zulu army was in hiding only a few kilometres from his own column. Leaving half his soldiers behind at a temporary camp close to Isandlwana Hill, the British Commander-in-Chief moved forward with the remainder of the column, his intention being to engage small parties of Zulus who had been reported to be in the area.

The officers who were being left behind suggested that defences should be built around the Isandlwana camp but no orders were given because Chelmsford considered the camp to be of a purely temporary nature. It proved a fatal error of military judgement.

Lieutenant Melvill was one of those at Isandlwana when on the morning of 22nd January, 1879, reports came in that Zulus had been seen nearby and the soldiers were given orders to stand-to. When nothing untoward happened immediately the order was rescinded.

In mid-morning Lieutenant Colonel Durnford of the Royal Engineers passed through the camp with a number of companies of native troops. After a brief stop he went on but had not progressed far beyond Isandlwana when he clashed with a party of Zulus. He swiftly realised that he was, in fact, fighting one of the 'horns' – or wings – of a Zulu formation and that it was in sufficient strength to seriously endanger the encampment he had only recently left.

He began to withdraw towards Isandlwana, his men fighting desperately, but the odds against the small force were far too great. They were overwhelmed and killed – and now the victorious Zulu impis could turn their full attention on the ill-prepared British encampment.

When the attack came, Colonel Pulleine, the officer commanding the 1st Battalion of the 24th Foot, who was in charge of the camp, quickly realised that his force stood little chance against the overwhelming might of the Zulu army and could not even retreat to safety. He ordered Lieutenant Teignmouth Melvill to break away from the battle in an attempt to prevent the battalion's Queen's Colour from falling into the hands of the enemy.

With the Colour contained in a leather case held across the pommel of his horse's saddle, Melvill left the camp, heading for the nearby Buffalo river, which formed the border between Zululand and Natal.

The whole area was swarming with armed Zulus and Melvill's red tunic made him an immediate target. Meanwhile, the men he had left behind were selling their lives dearly – but their situation was hopeless. All but a pitiful few would die at the hands of Cetshwayo's warriors.

On his way, Melvill had been joined by Lieutenant Nevill Coghill, an Irish fellow officer of the 24th Regiment, who until now had been kept out of much of the action because of an injured knee.

Closely pursued by Zulus, the two men reached the river and Coghill crossed safely. Unfortunately, Melvill, hampered by the Queen's Colour got into difficulties. Losing both horse and colour he was seen by Coghill to be clinging to a rock in mid-river, threatened by both the river and by Zulus.

Turning back, Coghill plunged into the river once more and succeeded in bringing Melvill to the Natal shore, even though his own horse was shot from beneath him by the pursuing Zulus.

But the Zulus had crossed the river too and although the two officers defended themselves as best they could, they were both doomed to suffer the fate of their comrades at Isandlwana.

In February 1879, two weeks after the disastrous battle, a British army patrol found the bodies of the two officers of the 24th close to the river, and they were interred in stone cairns at the place where they fell.

Incredibly, the Queen's Colour was also retrieved from the river and taken home to England later that same year.

In April, three months after the battle of Isandlwana, the bodies of Melvill and Coghill were exhumed and buried a short distance away. In due course their burial place was marked by a plaque and a stone cross and the place where they crossed the river was named 'Fugitives' Drift'.

A letter from Major General Dillon, on behalf of the Duke of Cambridge, Commander-in-Chief of the British army, was sent to Melvill's father, and would one day play an important part in ensuring that both Teignmouth and Lieutenant Coghill were accorded the recognition they so justly deserved.

Below is the letter dated 21st April 1879:

Sir,

I am directed by the Field Marshal Commanding in Chief to inform you that His Royal Highness perused with melancholy interest the report forwarded to him by Lord Chelmsford from Colonel Glyn, shewing how the queen's Color of the 1st Battalion 24th Foot would have fallen into the hands of the enemy on the 22nd January but for the gallant behaviour of your son, Lieutenant and Adjutant Melvill and Lieutenant Coghill of that Regiment. His Royal Highness in communicating this despatch to you desires me to assure you of his sincere sympathy with you in the loss of your son, whose gallant death in the successful endeavour to save the Color of his Regiment, has gained the admiration of the army.

It is gratifying to His Royal Highness to inform you that, if your son had survived his noble effort, it was Her Majesty's intention to confer upon him the Victoria Cross, and a notification to that effect will be made in the London Gazette.

I have the honor to be, Sir,
Your obedient Servant,
(signed) M.A. Dillon
Major General

Teignmouth Melvill's young widow had an audience with Queen Victoria and was granted a pension of £100 a year and their two sons were destined to have highly distinguished careers in the army.

Charles William Melvill commanded the 1st New Zealand Infantry Brigade at Gallipoli during the 1st World War, and was to become a Major General in charge of New Zealand Forces, being awarded the CB, CMG and DSO.

His brother, Colonel Teignmouth Philip Melvill, DSO, served in the South Wales Borderers and went on to command the 17th Lancers.

Lieutenant Teignmouth Melvill's posthumous Victoria Cross was gazetted on 15th January 1907 and was presented to Mrs Melvill later the same year. The VC is now in the possession of the Regimental Museum at Brecon.

There are a number of memorials to Teignmouth Melvill, VC. At Fugitives' Drift, Natal, South Africa; St Finbarre's Cathedral, Cork, Ireland; Harrow School Chapel and Cheltenham College.

But perhaps the most poignant memorial of all is the stained glass window in the tiny Cornish church of St Winnow, where Teignmouth Melvill and his wife would have worshipped with Teignmouth's family. Nearby, his father and mother lie in the peaceful churchyard, far removed from the bloody battleground where their heroic son met his end.

Theodore William Henry Veale 1892–1980

Heroes are not always immediately recognisable for what they are, no matter how courageous their deeds. They do not necessarily stand out in a crowd. Indeed, many who have been awarded a Victoria Cross give a first impression of gentleness and a meek demeanour that is at odds with their remarkable deeds of heroism.

One such man is Theodore Veale, who won a Victoria Cross on 20th July, 1916, when he was a stretcher bearer with the 8th Battalion of The Devonshire Regiment. The Battalion had been given orders to attack a heavily defended section of the German lines near Delville Wood, in France, during the early days of the bloody battle of the Somme, when the Battalion would lose more than a quarter of its strength.

Reinforced by a number of untried soldier straight from training in Great Britain, the target for the Devonshires was 'Wood Lane', a road that traversed a ridge covered with standing corn.

An Allied barrage began at 3.15am but unfortunately the initial shells fell short of their target, resulting in a number of casualties among the British troops waiting to go 'over the top'.

Worse was to follow. The Germans had positioned machine-guns to cover the area that would need to be traversed in just such an attack and they proved to be deadly effective.

In A and C Companies of the Devonshires all the officers were soon either killed or wounded and a company sergeant major and a corporal assumed command.

When news was received that one of the company commanders was lying wounded somewhere ahead of the Battalion's positions, Private Veale was one of those who went out to search for him.

Veale found the wounded officer lying in the corn – but he was less than ten metres from a German position. Nevertheless, although under enemy fire, he succeeded in dragging the officer a distance of about fifteen metres closer to the British lines and placing him in the doubtful security of a shell hole, before setting off to find water for the wounded man.

On his return, Private Veale tried to drag the officer closer to safety but, under continuous heavy fire, he was unsuccessful. Making the officer as

Theodore William Henry Veale

comfortable as was possible in the circumstances, he returned to the British lines to seek help.

Accompanied by a small party of soldiers, Veale located the British officer once more and they were moving him closer to their own lines when one of the party was shot and killed. The German rifle fire became so fierce that the surviving rescuers were forced to abandon the officer once more in another shell hole until darkness would make another rescue attempt possible.

In fact, dusk was just falling when Veale returned yet again, this time accompanied by a chaplain and a small party of stretcher bearers.

They succeeded in reaching the wounded officer – but then an enemy patrol was sighted creeping up on them. While one of the party attempted to keep the Germans at bay using a handgun, Veale ran back a hundred and fifty metres under heavy enemy fire, procured a Lewis gun and returned to the rescue scene.

With the Lewis gun he successfully kept the German patrol at bay, enabling the rescue party to successfully carry the wounded officer – a Lieutenant Edwin Savill – to safety.

For his actions on this day Theodore Veale was awarded a Victoria Cross and promoted to corporal.

The officer whose life was saved survived to become Sir Eric Savill, but Veale's future was less of a success story. After leaving the army he became so short of money that he was forced to put his medals up for sale in 1973. Fortunately, they were purchased by the Devonshire Regiment and are now on display in the Regimental Museum at the Keep, Dorchester.

One of the oldest surviving holders of the VC, Veale died at his home in Hoddesdon on November 6th, 1980, a few days short of his 88th birthday.

Theodore Veale was born in Dartmouth, Devon, in November 1892, his father a builder and his mother a professional concert pianist. Educated in Dartmouth schools, Theodore was a popular figure in his home town and was one of the first men in the area to volunteer for the army in the First World War.

The portrait of this gentle man now hangs in the officers' mess of the regiment he served so gallantly and Theodore Veale richly deserves his place among the bravest of the men who left the West Country to go to war.